Z4-Sp/2

Wills
OF THE
RICH AND
FAMOUS

Wills

OF THE RICH AND FAMOUS

COMPILED BY
HERBERT E. NASS

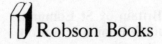
Robson Books

First published in Great Britain in 1991 by
Robson Books Ltd, Bolsover House, 5–6
Clipstone Street, London W1P 7EB

Copyright © 1991 Herbert E. Nass
The right of Herbert E. Nass to be identified
as author of this work has been asserted by
him in accordance with the Copyright,
Designs and Patents Act 1988

Book design by Giorgetta Bell McRee

**British Library Cataloguing in Publication
Data**
Nass, Herbert, E.
 Wills of the rich and famous
 1. Wills
 I. Title
 929.309

 ISBN 0 86051 746 2

Printed in Great Britain by St Edmunds-
bury Press Ltd, Bury St Edmunds, Suffolk

To the two most important women in my life:

My loving and beloved wife, Jodi,
whose support, hard work, and good cheer have been
constant sources of inspiration for me,

and

My beloved and loving mother, Edna,
whose spirit, appreciation of art, and good humor
helped me to be me.

Acknowledgments

So many people have been supportive of me and this endeavor, and I would like to thank them all. In particular, the following people deserve special thanks for their inspiration, assistance, and comments:

Seth and Liz Neubardt
Jim Miller
Beverly and Marvin Miller
Barry Schkolnick, Esq.
Harlan Stone
Ruth and Norman Stone
Michael Kaminsky, Esq.
Franklin Speyer
Henry Zimet
Martin Zimet
Donald and Shelley Meltzer
Harold Kushner
Dennis Fisher
Meredith and Jordan Berlin
Linda White
Sandy and Bud Neubardt
Phyllis and Fred Pressman
Dennis Massie
Richard Sarnoff
William Sarnoff
Mel Parker
Ruth, Linda, and Henry Nass
Karen Gantz Zahler, Esq.
Jeff Hoover
Vicki, Michael, and David Grossman

Robert Hayman
Robert Gries
Robert Sonnenblick
Tom Kornreich
Steven Lowy
Andy Kamins
Ken Leith
Lewis Rubin, Esq.
Ivan Jenson
Victor Matthews
J.S.G. Boggs
David Janis
Ken Bowen
Francis MacGrath
Greta and John Locksley
Amy and Brad Collins
Fred Hayman
Joe Nass, Esq.
Jerry Ordover, Esq.
Susan Frunzi, Esq.
Peter Ginsberg
Brian Lloyd Tell
Theodore Faro Gross
Alan Halperin, Esq.
Steven A. Ludsin, Esq.
Dan Troy, Esq.

Tom Danziger, Esq.
Anna Martinez
Kevin Brandon
Matthew Rich
Brandon Sall, Esq.
Lisa Beck
Harvey-Jane Kowal
Stacey Milbauer
David Jacoby, Esq.
Elaine Jacoby
William D. Zabel, Esq.
Dayna Langfan
Linda Rubin
Lesley Ann Gleidman
Stuart Hammer, C.P.A.
Larry and Claire
  Benenson
Laurence A. Tisch
David Nachman, Esq.
Burt and Leni Welte
Dan Lahat, Esq.
Andy and Jane Neubardt
Robert Steinberg, Esq.
Milton Levitan, Esq.
Randy Harris, Esq.
Steve Eckhaus, Esq.
Larry Lowenstein
Holly Reid

Dan Troy, Esq.
Steve Boldt
Larry Shire, Esq.
Rick Pappas, Esq.
Nancy Friedman
Geoff Trigger
David Simon, Esq.
Shelby Clark
William Levitt, C.P.A.
Louis Nizer, Esq.
Millard L. Midonick, Esq.
Herb Swartz, Esq.
Karen Davis
Susan Aminoff
John Good
Andy Hulsh, Esq.
Seth Jamison, Esq.
Francesca Jasper
Robert Strauss, Esq,
Andy Wallach
Amanda Neubardt
Daniel Ruben
Irwin Scherago, Esq.
Mort Rosenthal, Esq.
Steve Rosenberg, Esq.
Roger Olson, Esq.
Laura Foreman
Abraham Silberstein

And to Buck Finkelstein, Bernie Greene, Jack O'Neil, Mordie
Rochlin, David Washburn, Neale Albert, Robert Montgom-
ery, John Silberman, Simon Rifkind, Herbert Tenzer, Peter
Valente, Hal Daitch, Phil Michaels, Alan Brackman, Sidney
Mandel and Keith Nebel, all Esquires, who showed me how
law should be practiced, preached, and perhaps one day,
finally perfected.

Contents

Introduction

"Where There's a Will, There's a . . ."

A. Relative
B. Lawyer
C. Way
D. All of the above

With the personal lives of the rich and famous increasingly subject to public scrutiny, so, too, have their deaths and their Wills become a further subject of interest for the stargazing public. Knowing what a person directed or requested in his or her Will can shed light on that person's most private thoughts, feelings, and relationships. Each one of the sixty-odd Wills excerpted in this volume reflects interesting quirks, facts, or eccentric characteristics about the illustrious person who signed that Will.

"Thy will be done"
—John Greenleaf Whittier

For those who have prepared and signed their Wills, a Will can be used as a vehicle to express love or gratitude by giving property of value to specified surviving relatives, friends, or institutions. For example, actress **Marilyn Monroe** showed her devotion to her acting teacher, **Lee Strasberg**, by giving him all of her tangible personal property and 75 percent of her residuary estate to dispose of as *he* wished. Six years after Monroe's death, Strasberg showed his devotion to his third

1

wife, Anna, by giving her his entire estate, including his substantial continuing interest from the Monroe estate.

Gifts made under Wills need not be made only in cold cash, but may be of an object of special sentimental value. Ironically, comedian **Groucho Marx**, who once said that he would not want to be a member of any club that would have him, specifically bequeathed his membership in the Hillcrest Country Club in Beverly Hills to his son. Fittingly, comedian **W. C. Fields,** whose death was partly attributable to his excessive drinking, expressly gifted one-third of "my liquor" to each of three of his drinking buddies.

A Will may also be a person's last opportunity to vent pent-up emotions, settle a score, or set the record straight. The Will of actress **Joan Crawford** expressly disinherits two of her four children. Of course, one of those Crawford children who was "cut out" proceeded to write a best-selling book about life with her dear mommie.

Sometimes, a Will can be used to attempt to control the activities of surviving relatives "from the grave" by including bequests conditioned on the performance of specified conduct in the future. For example, pianist **Vladimir Horowitz** made a $300,000 gift to The Juilliard School of Music on the condition that Juilliard agrees "never to hold any piano or other musical competition in [Horowitz's] name or honor." That "strings attached" bequest was obviously made by one of music's most high-strung performers.

> **"With malice towards none, and charity for All . . . "**
> —Abraham Lincoln

Many of the Wills contained within include provisions for charities. Bequests made under Wills have often been the catalyst behind the establishment of great educational and medical institutions, museums, and private foundations. Billionaire **J. Paul Getty** gave most of his enormous estate toward the fulfillment of his dream to create a great museum bearing his name. In their Wills, artists **Mark Rothko, Andy Warhol, Norman Rockwell,** and **Robert Mapplethorpe** all created or funded private foundations to support the arts.

"To be of No Church is Dangerous"
—Samuel Johnson

A Will might also be seen as a person's last opportunity to prove his or her religious faith. In the first article of his Will, **J. P. Morgan** expressed the following deeply religious sentiments: "I commit my soul into the hands of my Saviour, in full confidence that having redeemed it and washed it in His most precious blood He will present it faultless before the throne of my Heavenly Father." Despite his tremendous success and wealth, perhaps Morgan was just hedging his bets and understood that "you can't take it with you."

"Let no one pay me honor with tears, nor celebrate my funeral with mourning"
—Cicero

Although lawyers usually advise against it because it may be too late when the Will is finally located, a Will can be used to give funeral, burial, cremation, or embalming instructions. Not surprisingly, many of our most public entertainers and movie stars specifically direct that their funerals be kept private and restricted to family members. In her Will, **Gloria Swanson** emphatically states: "I wish no public funeral or display of any sort. It is my wish that my body be cremated. I direct that my cremation be private and confined to members of my family only."

At the other extreme, some of our rich and famous dead took a very active role in planning their own funerals. **Cole Porter** requested that a certain biblical quotation he found especially comforting be read at his funeral. Great escape artist and magician **Harry Houdini** provided in his Will that his body should be embalmed and buried in a vault constructed in the same manner as his beloved mother's, and that a bronze bust of him be placed on his tomb so as to facilitate his projected return from the dead.

The Wills discussed in this book have been divided into the following eleven chapters: The Leading Ladies; The Leading Men; The Music Men; The Comedians; The Showmen; The Presidents; The Writers; The Producers and Directors; The Artists; One of a Kind; and last but certainly not least, The Super Rich.

The Leading Ladies have multiple husbands, romantic links to Clark Gable and two generations of Kennedys, star-struck mothers, and tragic deaths in common among them. **Marilyn Monroe, Jean Harlow, Carole Lombard,** and **Natalie Wood** all died tragic and untimely deaths. One might speculate as to whether such untimely deaths added to the legendary luster surrounding this subgroup of these ladies. Despite their deaths, these leading ladies will live forever on television screens and in movie theaters around the globe. Whether she be Harlow or Monroe, she is sometimes with us first thing in the morning, or on "The Late Show."

Our group of Leading Men appears to have been a hard-working bunch. Three of them had just completed filming movies shortly before they died. **Clark Gable** died two weeks after wrangling with horses and **Marilyn Monroe** on the set of *The Misfits*, **Spencer Tracy** had recently welcomed his daughter's fiancé, Sidney Poitier, to his home in *Guess Who's Coming to Dinner*, and **Henry Fonda** had acted with his daughter, Jane, in *On Golden Pond*. Shortly after Fonda received an Academy Award (in absentia) as Best Actor for his performance in that film, he went beyond Golden Pond.

The Music Men lived lives ranging from twenty-seven years in the case of rock singer **Jim Morrison** to the eighty-six years of concert pianist **Vladimir Horowitz**. As for their Wills, this select group of Music Men either paid little or no attention to their Wills or alternatively, focused their thoughts on their Wills. Rebel **Jim Morrison**'s Will was a one-pager, **Ricky Nelson**'s was three, and multimillionaire **John Lennon**'s was four. At the other extreme was songmaster **Cole Porter**, whose twenty-nine-page Will was prepared by one of New York's finest law firms and meticulously disposes of all his varied properties. **Elvis Presley** had a thirteen-page Will in which he gives broad discretion to his named executor, his father, Vernon Presley, to dispose of Elvis's "trophies" and other personal property.

Even the Comedians seem to take their own Wills seriously. There are no parting one-liners or any "magic words" in the Will of **Groucho Marx**. The Will of the tragically overdosed, burned-out "Saturday Night Live" comedian **John Belushi** is surprisingly and unusually structured, calculated, and family oriented. **Phil Silvers**'s handwritten Will and codicil read more like a rambling, intensely personal letter to family and friends than a legal document. Nonetheless, Silvers's stream-of-consciousness Will and codicil were admitted to probate by the California probate court.

The Wills of a few of the Showmen indicate their desire that the show involving them should go on after their deaths. **Harry Houdini** left specific instructions in his Will regarding his embalming and entombment, indicating his expectation that he would someday perform the ultimate trick and return from the dead. **Bob Fosse** wanted to be celebrated by sixty-six friends at numerous last suppers underwritten by Fosse's estate. **George M. Cohan's** Will gives a detailed discussion of the importance of his estate's retaining the copyrights to his lyrics and music, which would continue to produce income for his heirs long after he was gone.

Ranging from the one-sentence Will of taciturn **Calvin Coolidge** to the thirty-page, handwritten Will of the father of our country, **George Washington**, the Wills of the Presidents are representative of Wills of testators with comparable wealth and similar family situations. After all, even presidents put their pants on one leg at a time just like the rest of us. However, there is one important type of tangible personal property that only our presidents can claim as their own—presidential papers and other records associated with only the highest office in the land.

George Washington was of course the first to be concerned with the question of the proper disposition of his presidential records. **Thomas Jefferson** bequeathed his extensive library to the University of Virginia, and his "papers of business" passed to his executor for disposition. Coolidge's one-sentence Will makes no mention of any presidential papers. Perhaps the succinct Coolidge did not have too many papers of which to dispose. Despite its length and detailed attention to the disposition of his personal items, **Franklin Roosevelt's** Will is silent on the subject of the disposition of his presidential papers. Roosevelt died before any legislation related to the disposition of presidential papers was enacted. **John Kennedy's** Will, which was signed seven years *before* he became president and was never updated, obviously does not address the disposition of presidential papers. Kennedy's failure to update his Will after becoming president is somewhat odd in light of his brother Joseph's death at an early age, the substantial Kennedy family wealth, and the subsequent birth of Kennedy's two children, Caroline and "John-John." But what is even more perplexing is that Robert Kennedy, who was tragically assassinated in 1968 five years *after* his brother John, had an even older Will, dating back to 1953. Perhaps the Kennedy brothers shared some superstitions about signing their Wills; unfortunately, old Wills did not shield them from misguided assassins' new bullets.

A few of the Writers seemed to see their Wills as an opportunity to make some final comments on certain facts of life. For example, playboy **F. Scott Fitzgerald's** handwritten Will begins with a cynical allusion to "the uncertainty of life *and the certainty of death*" (emphasis added). Playwright **Lillian Hellman** used her Will as a stage to describe the background, sentimental and historical, of the various objects of tangible property that she was giving to selected friends. Most of these writers' Wills express their gratitude, and their egos, by bequests to various educational institutions or by the establishment of literary awards under their Wills, such as "The Truman Capote award for Literary Criticism in memory of Newton Arvin" or "The Dashiell Hammett Fund" established by Lillian Hellman.

In strange ways, the Wills of the Producers and Directors well reflect their creative styles. The one-page, handwritten Will of stark and truthful film director **John Cassavetes** minces no words and gets the job done in a direct, blunt manner. The Master of Suspense, **Alfred Hitchcock**, had a Will and then six subsequent changes to that Will by codicils spanning over seventeen years. Always controversial director **Orson Welles** makes a substantial gift to a woman who was not his wife. Romantic film-director **Vincente Minnelli** increased the bequest to his third wife by a codicil, but gives the bulk of his estate to his beloved daughter from his marriage to Judy Garland, Liza (With a Z) Minnelli. And **Walt Disney** seems to have had the all-American Will. From the starkness of Cassavetes's to the professional polish of Walt Disney's, the Wills of the Producers and the Directors display the temperaments of men who had already given many directions in the productions of their lives.

Inherently, estates of the Artists contain something that the rest of ours do not to the same extent—art. Very often, artists look at their artistic creations as their "children," so the final placement of their artworks takes on a profoundly personal meaning. For example, **Mark Rothko's** two-page Will mentions certain paintings for special disposition. Alternatively, in his relatively innocuous Will, pop artist **Andy Warhol** does not mention a single work of his art or anyone else's. Warhol's nine-page Will is certainly more polished than Rothko's two-pager, but both lacked the focused foresight required of persons disposing of exceptional estates. One other ironic fact that unites all of these artists is that as much as their work may have been admired during their lives, the value of their artworks increased dramatically after their deaths. Upon their deaths their artworks became a finite, fixed supply with the demand for that fixed supply significantly increased. Pop prophet **Andy Warhol** could not have been more correct when he said, "Death means a lot of money, honey."

In a universe all his own, brilliant scientist **Albert Einstein** left a Will in which his prized violin receives special treatment.

Last, but certainly not least under any criteria, are the Wills of the Super Rich. Almost every person written about in this book has been rich by most people's standards. But a few of our group of the Super Rich had fortunes counted in the billions of dollars. **J. Paul Getty** and **Howard Hughes** were billionaires before there were more than a handful of billionaires around. Hilton Hotels' commander and founder, **Conrad Hilton**, may not have been a billionaire, but he always knew that he could find a place to spend the night and get some room service.

As one might expect, the Wills of the Super Rich are often super long. It must be remembered that these Wills (with the notable exception of **Howard Hughes's**) were prepared by the attorneys for the Super Rich. No self-respecting attorney who expects to get paid a super fee would dare give a short Will to a Super Rich client. Every single contingency must be covered and accounted for, even it includes the notion in **Conrad Hilton's** Will that if every single one of his descendants and heirs conspired to contest his Will and lost, then the property would pass to the State of California.

J. Paul Getty's Will and the codicils to that Will win the prize for length. Getty's 1958 Will was a mere seventeen pages, but the aggregate of the twenty-one following codicils greatly exceeds that number. **Nelson Rockefeller's** Will was a princely sixty-four pages. As for mysterious **Howard Hughes**, if you added all the separate napkins, scraps of paper, and even legal paper that allegedly contained his Will, they might add up to something. In the end, they added up to nothing, and Hughes's billion-dollar estate passed by intestacy to Hughes's "laughing heirs," and to Uncle Sam.

It was first said by Benjamin Franklin that there are only two certainties in life—death and taxes. But for the Super Rich it may be said that there is only one certainty in life—death, but not necessarily taxes. By establishing private foundations or giving their fortunes exclusively to charity, these tremendous estates could avoid paying estate taxes. With the vast majority of **J. Paul Getty's** estate passing to the not-for-profit Getty Museum, there were relatively small estate taxes paid by his estate as a result of the unlimited charitable deduction available.

The Will excerpts reproduced in this book are the testators' or testatrices' (and lawyers') own words. In almost every case, except in the one-page Wills included here, the excerpted portions do not include the entire dispositive scheme, but only the sections of greatest interest. Entire sections of these Wills have been omitted or are not discussed due to an excess of "legalese" and a minimum of interesting material. Following are the excerpted highlights from the Wills of some of the most popular and celebrated people from the historical past and of our times.

THE LEADING LADIES

Diamonds to Dust

The Leading Lady	Date of Death
Jean Harlow Platinum Turns to Dust	June 7, 1937
Carole Lombard Till Death Do Us Part	January 17, 1942
Marilyn Monroe "Something's Got to Give"	August 5, 1962
Joan Crawford Whatever Happened to Baby Joan?	May 10, 1977
Natalie Wood West Coast Story	November 30, 1981
Gloria Swanson Sunset on Sunset Boulevard	April 4, 1983

Jean Harlow

Date and Place of Birth	Date and Place of Death
March 3, 1911 Kansas City, Missouri	June 7, 1937 Good Samaritan Hospital Hollywood, California

Platinum Turns to Dust

Born Harlean Carpenter in Kansas City, in 1927 at the age of sixteen, Harlean eloped with a Chicago bond broker named Charles McGrew 2d, and the couple moved to Beverly Hills, California. With her stunning platinum-blond hair and alluring sexuality, she began appearing on the silver screen under the name of Jean Harlow. However, it was not until after the date she signed her Will that she legally changed her name to Jean Harlow, according to papers filed by her mother with the Los Angeles court.

Seven months after moving to Hollywood, the McGrews separated and were subsequently divorced. Harlow's second husband, Paul Bern, committed suicide in 1932 two months after their marriage by shooting himself at home in Harlow's bedroom. In September of 1933, the actress married a cameraman named Harold G. Rosson, but in March 1935 the actress commenced a divorce action against him, complaining in part that his reading in bed did not allow her to receive the proper amount of rest.

It is noteworthy that the Will includes a "One Dollar ($1.00)" *in terrorem* clause enjoining anyone from contesting the Will. Based on her marital history, Harlow appears to have been terrifying indeed.

At the time of her death in 1937 at the age of twenty-six,

it was reported in *The New York Times* that Jean Harlow had an estate that was worth in excess of $1 million. After an illness of only a few days, she died of complications arising from uremic poisoning. At her bedside when she died was her fiancé, actor William Powell, and as one would expect, her mother and sole heir, Jean Harlow Bello.

Harlow was laid to rest in a crypt in a private sanctuary room in Glendale's Forest Lawn Cemetery. The room contained marble from France, Italy, and Spain and was reportedly purchased by Powell for $25,000 as a tribute to the woman he then loved. The second crypt in the room is occupied by the body of Harlow's number one fan—her mother.

/S/ Harlean Rosson

WILL DATED: September 5, 1935

Carole Lombard

Date and Place of Birth	Date and Place of Death
October 6, 1909	January 17, 1942
Fort Wayne, Indiana	Table Rock Mountain, Nevada

Till Death Do Us Part

Born Carol Jane Peters in Fort Wayne, Indiana, Carole (who added an e to her name when she adopted her stage name) Lombard became one of the brightest stars in Hollywood.

In 1931, Lombard was married to her costar in *My Man Godfrey*, William Powell, but that marriage lasted only two years before ending in divorce. In 1939, Miss Lombard married film star Clark Gable, and the couple were reported to be among Hollywood's happiest at the time of Miss Lombard's tragic death three years later.

As indicated in her Will dated August 8, 1939, Carole Lombard left her entire estate to her husband, Clark Gable, and named him as the sole executor. For the provisions of the Will of Clark Gable, who died eighteen years later in 1960, see page 37 of this volume.

Carole Lombard's death came suddenly and tragically when the airplane in which she, her mother, and twenty others were flying crashed and burned near Las Vegas, Nevada. In light of her fiery end, it is indeed ironic that the first article of Lombard's Will provides the following:

> I request that no person other than my immediate family and the persons who shall prepare my remains for

interment be permitted to view my remains after death
has been pronounced. I further request a private funeral and that I be clothed in white and placed in a
modestly priced crypt in Forest Lawn Memorial Park,
Glendale, California.

The search party that located all of the crash victims included cowboys, Indians, and soldiers. Miss Lombard's body
was not initially recognizable because it was so badly burned
and was only identified with the aid of dental records and
from a wisp of her blond hair. It is not known whether she
was "clothed in white" before being placed in a "modestly
priced" crypt at Forest Lawn Memorial Park cemetery as she
had requested in her Will.

When the remarried Clark Gable died in 1960, his body
was placed in the crypt next to the one holding his former
wife's remains. (Where Gable's fifth wife, to whom he was
married when he died, is buried is another story.) It was death
that brought the King and Queen of Hollywood back together
again.

/S/ *Carole Lombard*

WILL DATED: August 8, 1939

Marilyn Monroe

Date and Place of Birth	Date and Place of Death
June 1, 1926	August 5, 1962
Los Angeles General Hospital	12305 Fifth Helena Drive
Los Angeles, California	Los Angeles, California

"Something's Got to Give"

 *D*ead from an overdose of sleeping pills at age thirty-six, Marilyn Monroe became an international symbol of glamour and sex who commanded the attention of presidents, Pulitzer Prize–winning playwrights, and all-star ballplayers.

When Marilyn Monroe signed her Will on January 14, 1961, she was already divorced from three husbands, including base-ball legend Joe DiMaggio and playwright Arthur Miller. She had first been married at age sixteen to an aircraft worker named James Dougherty. Monroe had also been romantically linked with the Kennedy family. None of her three marriages or other liaisons produced any children, but there were re-portedly some close calls. Speaking of calls, there is provoc-ative evidence of a flurry of telephone calls from Monroe's home to Robert Kennedy's Justice Department office in the days just before her death.

Not surprisingly, Monroe's career was at its lowest ebb at the time of her suicide in 1962. Her last two films, *Let's Make Love* and *The Misfits* (written by her soon to be ex-husband Arthur Miller and co-starring Clark Gable shortly before his own death), had been commercial failures. Monroe had been dismissed from the set of *Something's Got to Give* two months before her death.

It has been reported that both Monroe's mother and grand-mother were committed to mental institutions during their lives. Article five of Monroe's Will establishes a $100,000 trust for "the maintenance and support of my mother, GLADYS BAKER," and another relative.

The remaining portion of that trust and 25 percent of the residuary estate is left to Monroe's psychotherapist, Dr. Marianne Kris, "to be used by her for the furtherance of the work of such psychiatric institutions or groups as she shall elect." When Dr. Kris died in 1980, she left her share of the Monroe estate to an institution that subsequently became the London-based Anna Freud Centre for the Psychoanalytic Study and Treatment of Children.

The largest portion of Marilyn Monroe's estate was left to the man she seemed to revere the most shortly before her death, legendary "method" acting teacher Lee Strasberg. Monroe displays her trust and faith in Strasberg by the following bequest of her personal property:

> I give and bequeath all of my personal effects and clothing to LEE STRASBERG, or if he should predecease me, then to my Executor hereinafter named, it being my desire that he distribute these, in his sole discretion, among my friends, colleagues and those to whom I am devoted.

Monroe's own devotion to Strasberg is evident from her substantial gift of "the entire remaining balance," or 75 percent, of her estate that Strasberg received under the following residuary clause of her Will:

> All the rest, residue and remainder of my estate . . . I give, devise and bequeath as follows:
> (a) to MAY REIS the sum of $40,000.00 or 25% of the total remainder of my estate, whichever shall be the lesser.
> (b) to DR. MARIANNE KRIS 25% of the balance thereof, to be used by her as set forth in ARTICLE FIFTH
> (d) of this my Last Will and Testament.

(c) to **LEE STRASBERG** the entire remaining balance.

It has been reported that the Monroe estate is continuing to earn income in excess of $1 million over twenty-five years after her death, through the licensing of her image on selected products and through film royalties. When Strasberg himself died in 1982, his share of the Monroe estate passed under his Will (see page 185 for excerpts from Strasberg's Will) to his surviving widow, Anna Strasberg. Strasberg had married Anna in 1968, six years *after* the death of Monroe.

As the primary beneficiary of the Monroe estate, Anna was recently named the sole administrator of it after the death of Monroe's named executor and the draftsman of her Will, attorney Aaron R. Frosch. One has to wonder whether Marilyn would truly have wanted her estate to pass to Strasberg's widow or the Anna Freud Centre in London. But in the end, Monroe may not have had anyone else whom she wanted to have it.

Monroe's body was finally laid to rest in the "Corridor of Memories" in the Westwood Village, California, Memorial Park cemetery. According to employees of that cemetery, Monroe's ex-husband Joe DiMaggio placed red roses on Monroe's crypt for many years after her death. However, despite persistent rumors, the unoccupied crypt right next to the one in which Monroe was laid is not owned in the name of Joe DiMaggio and may be available for purchase from the owner at a cost of approximately $50,000. For that price, one can lie next to the immortal remains of the most illustrious sex goddess of our times for an eternity. That is much longer than any of Monroe's ex-husbands made it.

/S/ *Marilyn Monroe*

WILL DATED: January 14, 1961

Joan Crawford

Date and Place of Birth	Date and Place of Death
March 23, 1908 San Antonio, Texas	May 10, 1977 150 East 69th Street New York, New York

Whatever Happened to Baby Joan?

Actress Joan Crawford appeared in over eighty movies, including her first screen success, *Our Dancing Daughters*, in 1928 and her shocking thriller *Whatever Happened to Baby Jane?* in 1962. Crawford was one of Hollywood's most glamorous movie queens, but behind the glamour, Crawford apparently had stormy relationships with three of her four husbands and at least two of her four adopted children.

Crawford's three marriages to actors Douglas Fairbanks, Jr., Franchot Tone, and Phillip Terry all ended in divorce. In 1955 she married Alfred N. Steele, who was the chairman and chief executive officer of the Pepsi-Cola Company. In 1959, Steel died of a heart attack. Steel's widow, Crawford, served on the Pepsi Board of Directors until she herself died of a heart attack eighteen years later in 1977.

During her four marriages, Crawford never bore any children. Instead, she adopted four children—Cathy, Cynthia, Christina, and Christopher. From her Will it appears that Crawford had good relationships with only two of her four children. The second-to-last article of her will states bluntly:

> It is my intention to make no provision herein for my son Christopher or my daughter Christina for reasons which are well known to them.

In her book entitled *Mommie Dearest,* Crawford's daughter Christina Crawford Koontz describes her reaction when she first saw those words in the Will that her mother had signed only seven months before her death: "My first impression was that these words she'd ordered put into her Last Will and Testament were from over twenty years ago. . . . She had tried to reach out of her grave and slap me one last time, just to prove who had really been in control all these years. . . . I was speechless and stunned. Not because of the money. It would have been a nice gesture, but it wasn't the money. It was the insult." *Mommie Dearest* also states that until she was legally adopted by the unmarried Crawford in Las Vegas, Nevada, at the age of eleven months, Christina's name had been Joan Crawford, Jr.

However, Crawford's two favored daughters, Cathy and Cynthia, did not receive too much to write home about either. It appears that daughter Cathy was number one in Crawford's heart as she is given all of Crawford's tangible personal property, if she survived. If she did not survive her mother, the tangible personal property was to go to daughter Cynthia. Furthermore, for daughters Cathy and Cynthia the Will establishes trust funds in the amount of $77,500 for each of them, with principal payments to be gradually doled out as follows until they each reached the age of fifty.

If such daughter shall have attained the following age at the time of my death:	I give and bequeath outright to her the following amount:
30 years	$5,000
35 years	15,000
40 years	30,000
45 years	45,000

I give and bequeath the remaining portion of the amount set apart for such daughter, or the entire amount set apart for her if she shall not have attained the age of 30 years at the time of my death, to my trustees hereinafter named in trust.

For each of the children of only these two daughters, Crawford made $5,000 bequests. There are also seven bequests ranging from $5,000 to $35,000, totaling $70,000, to employees and friends but to no other relatives.

Crawford divided her residuary estate into eight shares to be used for the general purposes of six named charities: the Muscular Dystrophy Association of America, the American Cancer Society, the American Heart Association, the Wiltwyck School for Boys, the USO of New York City, and the Motion Picture Country Home & Hospital. The Motion Picture Country Home received three of the eight shares and the other charities each received one share.

As one might have expected, cut-out daughter Christina and son Christopher chose to contest their mother's Will. According to an Agreement of Compromise filed with the New York Surrogate's Court, Christina and Christopher agreed to settle their claim against the estate for a total of $55,000 (less their attorney's fees). In addition, it was agreed that one plaster bust of the deceased Crawford inscribed "To Christina" would be delivered to her.

We need not be too concerned about the plight of Christina because the cover of the latest edition of her book *Mommie Dearest* proclaims that it has sold over 3 million copies. Ironically, Christina may have profited more from her exposé than her two sisters favored under their mother's Will.

The last article of Crawford's Will simply states: "I direct that my remains be cremated." Crawford's funeral took place on Friday the thirteenth, in May of 1977, but the bad luck may have begun long before then.

/S/ Joan Crawford Steele

WILL DATED: October 28, 1976

Natalie Wood

Date and Place of Birth

July 20, 1938
San Francisco, California

Date and Place of Death

November 30, 1981
Water off Santa Catalina
California

West Coast Story

*B*orn Natasha Gurdin to Russian immigrant parents in San Francisco, Natalie Wood got her new name at age six. Wood was one of the few child stars of Hollywood who successfully made the transition to adult film roles, including roles in *Rebel Without a Cause, Marjorie Morningstar,* and *West Side Story.*

Wood married actor Robert Wagner in 1957, was divorced from him in 1962, and then remarried him in 1972. Between her marriages to Mr. Wagner, she was also married to, and subsequently divorced from, English film producer Richard Gregson. Her marriage to Mr. Gregson produced a daughter named Natasha Gregson. Her second marriage to Mr. Wagner produced another daughter, Courtney Brooke Wagner. At the outset of her Will Wood expressly describes her family relationships as follows:

> I declare that I am married, and that my husband's name is ROBERT J. WAGNER. I have one child by a previous marriage, namely my daughter, NATASHA GREGSON, who was born September 29, 1970, and one child by my present marriage, namely my daughter, COURTNEY BROOKE WAGNER, who was born March 9, 1974. My said husband has one child by a previous marriage, namely his daughter KATHARINE WAGNER, who was born May 11, 1964.

Later in the Will, Natalie Wood provides that husband Robert should be the guardian of her daughter Natasha from her prior marriage and expressly states her reasons for doing so as follows:

> Under circumstances now existing, I feel that in the event that I am survived by my husband, ROBERT J. WAGNER, the best interest of my daughter NATASHA would be served if he were appointed guardian of her person and estate. My husband has assured me that in · such event he would cooperate with NATASHA's father in the same manner that I would cooperate with him in maintaining his relationship with NATASHA. Accordingly it is my desire and request that ROBERT J. WAGNER be appointed to serve in those capacities. ... Accordingly, in the event that both my husband and I are deceased during the minority of my daughter COURTNEY, it is my desire and request that she and NATASHA be raised together in the same household, in California, and that they be cared for by my housekeeper WILLIE MAE WORTHEN.

The role of mother was evidently important to her, as Wood singles out one painting she owned entitled *The Three Ages of Motherhood* for special disposition under her Will.

To her sister Olga Viripaeff, Wood made a bequest of $15,000, and she gave to her sister "LANA GURDIN, also known as LANA WOOD, all of my furs and clothing." To her husband, Robert Wagner, Wood left "all of my interest in automobiles, household furnishings, paintings and other works of art (except as hereinafter provided), jewelry and remaining personal effects" and a portion of her residuary estate. The balance of her residuary estate was to be held in trust for the benefit of her parents and children. Wagner was appointed the executor and trustee of his wife's Will.

Natalie Wood signed her Will about a year and a half prior

to her tragic drowning near Santa Catalina Island off the coast of Los Angeles. At the time of her death, she had been cruising on a fifty-five-foot cabin cruiser with her husband, Robert Wagner, and actor Christopher Walken, who was costarring with Wood in a film entitled *Brainstorm*. After a seven-hour search by the Coast Guard, Wood's body was found in a rocky cove near Santa Catalina. Her death was called an accidental drowning by investigators.

Wood is buried in the Westwood Village Memorial Park, a short distance from the crypt of another West Coast girl, named Marilyn Monroe.

/S/ Natalie Wagner

WILL DATED: April 17, 1980

Gloria Swanson

Date and Place of Birth	Date and Place of Death
March 27, 1899 Chicago, Illinois	April 4, 1983 New York Hospital New York, New York

Sunset on Sunset Boulevard

The only child of Joseph and Adelaide Svensson, Gloria May Josephine Svensson was born in Chicago in 1899. Gloria Svensson adopted the name "Swanson," and she became the glittering goddess of Hollywood's roaring twenties. Ms. Swanson summed up her larger-than-life presence in films with her famous line in the 1950 film *Sunset Boulevard:* "I *am* big. It's the movies that got small."

By the time of her death, Gloria Swanson had been married six times and divorced five times. Her last marriage was in 1976 to writer William Dufty, but he receives nothing under her Will. Early in her career, she was also romantically linked with a Boston financier and patriarch of an American political dynasty, Joseph P. Kennedy.

Her six marriages produced two daughters, Gloria Daly and Michelle Amon, and she adopted a son, Joseph, who predeceased her in 1977. She named her two daughters and her attorney as executors of her Will. Her Will divides her estate to give 40 percent to each of her daughters and 10 percent to each of the surviving daughters of her predeceased son as follows:

...I give, devise and bequeath all the rest residue and remainder of my Estate, real, personal or mixed and wherever situated as follows:

(a) Forty percent (40%) to my daughter, GLORIA S. DALY of...New York City....

(b) Forty percent (40%) to my daughter, MICHELLE AMON of Neuilly, 92200 France....

(c) Ten percent (10%) to my granddaughter CHRISTINA SWANSON and ten percent (10%) to my granddaughter PATRICIA SWANSON.

However, a subsequent codicil to the Will executed in 1981 inexplicably drastically changes the disposition of the residuary estate, providing that daughter Gloria would receive the odd percentage of 13⅓ of her mother's estate outright, and the other 26⅔ of her 40-percent share was to be held in trust for the benefit of Swanson's *other* daughter, Michelle. Daughter Michelle continued to received 40 percent of her mother's estate outright.

Swanson was known for her extravagance and lavish lifestyle. It is reported that she earned $8 million between 1918 and 1929 and that she spent nearly all of that. When she died at the age of eighty-four, her gross estate was in excess of $1,440,000 according to papers filed with the New York court.

The first article of the Will directs that Swanson's cremation be private and confined to members of her family only and that there be "no public funeral or display of any sort." Dead in her eighties, the shining star of the twenties guarded her image until the very end.

/S/ Gloria Swanson

WILL DATED: March 4, 1981
CODICIL DATED: September 11, 1981
Residing at 920 Fifth Avenue, New York, New York

THE LEADING MEN

Last Curtain Calls

The Leading Man	Date of Death
Douglas Fairbanks The Public Life of Don Juan	December 12, 1939
Humphrey Bogart Cigarette Smoking Was Hazardous to His Health	January 14, 1957
Clark Gable Gone With the Wind	November 16, 1960
Spencer Tracy Guess Who's Not Coming to Dinner	June 10, 1967
Edward G. Robinson The End of Rico	January 26, 1973
John Wayne Put Down Your Dukes	June 11, 1979
William Holden Sunset on Ocean Avenue	November 16, 1981

Henry Fonda   August 12, 1982
Beyond Golden Pond

Rock Hudson   October 2, 1985
Bad Day at Castle Rock

Cary Grant   November 29, 1986
He Was No Angel

Douglas Fairbanks

Date and Place of Birth	Date and Place of Death
May 23, 1883 Denver, Colorado	December 12, 1939 705 Ocean Front Santa Monica, California

The Public Life of Don Juan

One of the greatest stars of the silent-film era, Douglas Fairbanks was known worldwide for his roles as Robin Hood, the Thief of Baghdad, Don Q., and Don Juan. Fairbanks, who had a smile that charmed the world, was married three times, first to Beth Sully in New York in 1907. That marriage ended in divorce in 1919. In 1920, Fairbanks married screen star Mary Pickford in Los Angeles in a wedding that was one of the most sensational Hollywood had ever seen, and their home in Beverly Hills, dubbed "Pickfair," was reportedly out of this world. It seems that the Fairbanks-Pickford relationship lost its magic in the mid-1930s; they were finally divorced on January 14, 1936. After their divorce, Pickford remained at Pickfair and lived there with her next husband until her death in 1979.

On March 7, 1936, in Paris, Fairbanks married Lady Ashley, former wife of London's Lord Ashley and formerly a musical comedy actress named Sylvia Hawkes.

In his Will dated November 2, 1936, Fairbanks leaves 20/40ths of his estate to his "beloved wife, SYLVIA FAIRBANKS," with the provision that such amount shall not exceed $1 million. He leaves 12/40ths to his "beloved son DOUGLAS FAIRBANKS, JR.," but not to exceed $600,000. Two-fortieths are left to his "beloved brother" Robert Fairbanks, but not

31

to exceed $100,000, and one-fortieth to his "beloved brother" Norris Wilcox. One-fortieth of the estate equal to $50,000 was placed in trust for each of Fairbanks's four nieces, and the final fortieth ("not to exceed the sum of Fifty Thousand Dollars ($50,000.00)"), was left to Douglas Fairbanks, Jr., "absolutely but with the request that he distribute said sum to the people and in the proportions as I advise him by letter addressed to him to be found with this Will." The contents of that letter were never revealed. Any property remaining after the foregoing fractional amounts were paid was to be divided equally between Fairbanks's wife, Sylvia, and son, Douglas, Jr.

The Will also provides for a $10,000 bequest to the Motion Picture Actors' Relief Fund of Los Angeles, California, to be known as the "Douglas Fairbanks Fund." Fairbanks named the Bank of America National Trust & Savings Association as executor of his Will for property located in California, and the Guaranty Trust Company of New York "as Executor to administer upon all of my estate located outside the State of California." It is unusual to appoint two different executors to administer different property, but Fairbanks liked to do things his way.

Fairbanks died of a sudden heart attack at the age of fifty-six while sleeping in his home overlooking the Pacific Ocean in Santa Monica, California. After Fairbanks's death, it was reported that Fairbanks's 150-pound mastiff named Marco Polo whined for hours near Fairbanks's bed, refusing to move after his master's death. Apparently, the famed Fairbanks smile affected fans not only of the human species.

/S/ *Douglas Fairbanks*

WILL DATED: November 2, 1936

Humphrey Bogart

Date and Place of Birth

December 25, 1899
West 103rd Street
New York, New York

Date and Place of Death

January 14, 1957
Holmby Hills, California

Cigarette Smoking Was Hazardous to His Health

Dead from throat cancer at the age of fifty-seven, actor
Humphrey Bogart appeared in many screen classics and made
Casablanca famous. Despite his often brusque style and tough-
guy image, Humphrey Bogart was apparently also very lovable, being married to four different actresses. He divorced
his first wife, Helen Menken, in 1927 after one year of marriage. His subsequent marriage to Mary Phillips lasted until
1937. In 1938, Bogart married Mayo Methot. Mayo finally
allowed Bogart to obtain a Nevada-style divorce from her in
1945. Shortly after that, Bogart married his *To Have and Have
Not* costar, actress Lauren Bacall. Bacall was still happily married to Bogart when he died twelve years later.

The first article of Bogart's Will, which he signed in 1956
about six months before he died, states:

> I am married to Betty Bogart (also known as LAUREN
> BACALL BOGART) and have two children, namely, my
> son STEPHEN HUMPHREY BOGART, who was born
> January 6, 1949, and my daughter LESLIE BOGART,
> who was born August 23, 1952.

To his wife "Betty," as Bogart affectionately referred to her, he left all of his "clothing and personal effects ... jewelry, automobiles and accessories thereto, and such interest as I may have in household furniture, furnishings, equipment and effects of every sort and nature." If his wife did not survive him, then Bogart provided that his friend and business manager, A. Morgan Maree, Jr., should dispose of the property "in such manner as he may believe would comply with my desires." Mr. Maree, who was a trusted adviser to both Humphrey and Betty Bogart, was also named as co-executor of the Will, together with Betty Bogart and the Security-First National Bank of Los Angeles. For her own reasons, Betty declined to serve as an executor of her husband's estate according to papers filed with the court, but she did serve as a trustee of her children's trusts.

In his Will, Bogart places one-half of his residuary estate in trust for his wife, "Betty." That trust provides:

> The purpose of this trust shall be to provide for the security and welfare of my beloved wife BETTY during the remainder of her life. In establishing this trust I am particularly aware of her high earning potential, the impact of income taxes thereon, the standard of living to which she has been accustomed during our marriage, and the uncertainties of the many years during which I hope her life will continue in the event of my decease.

The balance of Bogart's estate was to be held in trust for his two children until they reached the age of forty-five. The trustees had the discretion to invade principal or income for his children's benefit, and in this regard the Will states:

> In exercising such discretion my trustees shall take into account the provisions that my wife BETTY shall be able to make for such child from time to time out of

funds available to her and shall be guided as near as may be by the standard of living to which said children have been accustomed during my lifetime. It is my desire that their care, comfort and welfare be adequately provided for during their tender years, that they be afforded every opportunity for such higher education as may be appropriate in view of their interest and ability, and that consideration for their support and maintenance after completion of their education shall be secondary.

If neither Betty nor any children survived, there were provisions for "BETTY's mother, NATALIE GOLDBERG, so long as she shall live, and thereafter in equal shares to BETTY's cousins, JUDITH DAVIS ORSHAN and JOAN DAVIS." Just for the record, Bacall's mother, Natalie Goldberg, lived on Cranberry Street in Brooklyn, New York.

In addition to providing for his wife's family, Bogart also makes modest bequests to two of his employees. Finally, the Will also includes an unusual clause in which any persons claiming to be heirs of Bogart would receive only a $1.00 bequest.

One screen habit that Bogart has come to be identified with is smoking cigarettes. The cigarette dangling from the mouth is probably more closely identified with Bogart than with any other actor in history. It is not then surprising that Bogart died of cancer of the esophagus at the relatively young age of fifty-seven. Nor is it then surprising that the one charitable bequest that Bogart makes in his Will is as follows:

If the circumstances shall ever be such that THE HUMPHREY BOGART FOUNDATION shall become entitled to receive any property... I direct my trustees to cause to be formed a nonprofit corporation bearing that name to receive such property. Said corporation shall have as its primary purpose the making of grants for the aid

of medical research, with special reference to the field
of cancer. [emphasis added]

One wonders whether if Bogart had known that the cigarette
habit would be hazardous to his health (and that of millions
of others), he would have been so willing to use the cancer
stick as a prop throughout his career.

/S/ Humphrey Bogart

WILL DATED: June 6, 1956
Residing at 232 S. Mapleton Drive, Los Angeles, California

Clark Gable

Date and Place of Birth

February 1, 1901
Cadiz, Ohio

Date and Place of Death

November 16, 1960
Hollywood Presbyterian Hospital
Hollywood, California

Gone With the Wind

Called "the King of Hollywood," Clark Gable starred as southern gentleman Rhett Butler in the 1939 screen classic *Gone With the Wind* and in the ill-fated *The Misfits* with Marilyn Monroe shortly before they both died. Known as the consummate lady-killer, Gable did not appear to be too lucky in love. He was married five times. His first marriage, to Josephine Dillon, ended in divorce in 1930. His second marriage, to Rhea Langham, ended in divorce in 1939. His third marriage ended tragically when his wife, actress Carole Lombard, was killed in a plane crash on January 17, 1942. Gable and Lombard were reported to have had one of Hollywood's happiest marriages. It is noteworthy that after his death eighteen years later, Gable's body was placed in a crypt next to that of his former wife. One has to wonder how Gable's fifth and final wife, Kay, felt about where husband Clark was finally laid to rest.

After the plane crash killing Carole Lombard, Gable joined the United States Air Force and became a private at the age of forty-one. Gable flew in dangerous combat bombing missions over Europe, and with those war stories behind him, Clark Gable made a triumphant return to Hollywood.

After his return Gable married Lady Sylvia Ashley in 1949, but that marriage ended in divorce in 1952. In 1955, Gable married Kathleen ("Kay") Williams Spreckles, a model and actress, and he was married to her when he died of a heart attack at the age of 59 in 1960. It has been claimed that the tension on the set of *The Misfits* between the tardy Marilyn Monroe and her playwright (and soon to be ex-) husband, Arthur Miller, partially contributed to the emotional and physical strain on Gable.

Gable's last Will, which he signed in 1955, is just over two pages long and initially states, "I hereby declare that I am married to Kathleen G. Gable and that I have no children." Next, there is evidence of the gentleman Gable was known to be, as shown by a very unusual gift. To "JOSEPHINE DILLON, my former wife," Gable devised a piece of real property and a house located in North Hollywood, California. One doesn't usually see gifts to former wives in Wills, but Gable did it in his. Other than that one piece of property, Gable gave all the rest of his estate "to my beloved wife, KATHLEEN G. GABLE" and appointed her as the sole executrix of his Will. Perhaps as a precaution against the former wives who were not mentioned, Gable's Will also includes a $1.00 *in terrorem* clause.

Despite five marriages, Gable never had any children while he was alive. However, papers filed with the Los Angeles court reveal that Gable's wife, Kathleen, was pregnant with a child at the time of his death, referred to in the court papers as "Unborn Baby Gable." John Clark Gable was born on March 20, 1961, in the same hospital in which his father had died 124 days earlier.

/S/ *Clark Gable*

WILL DATED: September 19, 1955

Spencer Tracy

Date and Place of Birth

April 5, 1900
Milwaukee, Wisconsin

Date and Place of Death

June 10, 1967
9191 St. Ives Drive
Beverly Hills, California

Guess Who's Not Coming to Dinner

Appearing in over sixty films during his long career, Spencer Tracy won the Academy Award for Best Actor two years in a row but may be best known for his appearances in nine films with Katharine Hepburn, with whom he was romantically linked. Hepburn and Tracy's final appearance together was in Tracy's last movie, *Guess Who's Coming to Dinner*, which was completed shortly before he died.

Mr. Tracy, who was a devout Catholic, had married an actress named Louise Treadwell in 1923. Despite his romance with Ms. Hepburn, Spencer remained married to Louise until death did them part. As his Will states, the Tracys had two children.

> I am married. My wife is LOUISE TREADWELL TRACY.
> I have two children, the issue of our marriage, a son,
> JOHN TEN-BROECK TRACY, and a daughter, LOUISE
> TREADWELL TRACY, also known as SUSIE TRACY.

John was born totally deaf in 1924. As a result of his son's deafness, Tracy and his wife founded the John Tracy Clinic for the Deaf in Los Angeles in 1942.

In his 1961 Will, Tracy makes the following bequests of his tangible personal property:

FOURTH: I bequeath all of my jewelry to my daughter, Susie, and to my son, John, to be divided as they may agree.

FIFTH: I bequeath to my brother, CARROLL E. TRACY, that automobile owned by me and used by me as my personal automobile, whichever automobile that shall be at the time of my death. I further bequeath to my said brother my wardrobe, or such part thereof as he selects....

SIXTH: I devise and bequeath to my wife, Louise Tracy, my interest in our residence or residences and such item or items as she may select from my remaining articles of personal, domestic or household use or ornament, including my remaining automobiles.

In the codicil to his Will, which he executed about two years later, Tracy revoked article five of his Will and substituted the following:

FIFTH: I bequeath to my brother, CARROLL E. TRACY, all of the furniture, fixtures, paintings and other articles of ornament and household use at 9191 St. Ives Drive, Los Angeles, California, and the two automobiles owned by me and used by me for my personal use which are kept at said address. I further bequeath to my said brother my wardrobe, or such part thereof as he selects....

This change increased the property passing to Tracy's brother and at the same time reduced the tangible personal property passing to Tracy's wife. However, that same codicil changed the distribution of Tracy's residuary estate so that one-half was to be distributed outright to his wife and the balance held in trust for her benefit, rather than the entire amount's being held in trust as the Will had provided. Seems as if Tracy did not want his wife to get her hands on his "wardrobe," automobiles, or "other articles of ornament and household use."

When he died, Tracy had not been living with his estranged wife. After learning that Tracy had been stricken by a heart attack at his home at six A.M., Tracy's brother, Carroll, arrived with a doctor, but it was too late. Arriving at Tracy's house soon thereafter were Tracy's wife, daughter, and son. Next came Tracy's longtime "companion" Katharine Hepburn, director George Cukor (who had been a witness to Tracy's Will), and Tracy's business manager, Ross Evans. Tracy's funeral was attended by many of Hollywood's notables, including Gregory Peck, Edward G. Robinson, and Frank Sinatra. However, conspicuously absent from Tracy's funeral was his favorite co-star, Katharine Hepburn.

/S/ *Spencer Tracy*

WILL DATED: May 6, 1961
CODICIL DATED: October 23, 1963

Edward G. Robinson

Date and Place of Birth	Date and Place of Death
December 12, 1893 Bucharest, Rumania	January 26, 1973 Mount Sinai Hospital Hollywood, California

The End of Rico

When he was born in Rumania, he was named Emanuel Goldenberg, but after his family emigrated to the United States, young Emanuel quickly mastered the English language and changed his name to the American-sounding Edward G. Robinson. Robinson's most famous role was that of Little Caesar in the 1931 film by that name in which he uttered his classic line after being shot by the police: "Mother of God, is this the end of Rico?"

In 1927, Robinson had married actress Gladys Lloyd. That marriage lasted for twenty-eight years before ending in divorce in 1955. In 1958, while appearing on Broadway and playing an older man who marries a much younger woman, Robinson married a thirty-eight-year-old woman named Jane Arden.

During his life, Robinson was known to be a serious collector of artworks. During the aftermath of his divorce, in 1957, Robinson reportedly sold the bulk of his art collection for $3,250,000. However, it appears there were still at least a few valuable paintings remaining, as the Will provides:

DISPOSITION OF PAINTINGS

A. If I am survived by my wife, JANE, I give and bequeath my painting by Pisarro [*sic*] entitled "The Dead

Tree", my painting by Vuillard of an interior scene with child in red dress entitled "Madame Vuillard au Dejeuner", my painting by Berthe Morisot entitled "Avant le Theatre" and all paintings painted by me (other than the portrait of my friend, Sam Jaffe) to my Trustees hereinafter named, in trust....

Finally, Robinson alludes to the prominence and future provenance of his art collection by stating:

I also recommend that my Executors or Trustees consider the possibility of conducting a sale of such paintings and other art objects at public auction under the most advantageous terms available; further, I suggest that such public auction might be held at Sotheby in London, unless in the light of all circumstances and conditions existing at that time it appears advantageous to conduct the sale at the Parke-Bernet Galleries, Inc. of New York City or Christies in London. It is my further belief that it would be proper and advantageous to sell my paintings and other art objects as "THE EDWARD G. ROBINSON COLLECTION."

Besides paintings, Robinson also appears to have been a collector of books, and for his beloved books he made the following provisions in his Will:

If I am survived by my wife, JANE, I give and bequeath all of my books to my said wife. If my said wife shall predecease me, then I direct that said books be distributed to my Trustees hereinafter named and that my Trustees retain said books for a period of two years from the time of my death. If, at the end of said two year period, my son, EDWARD, is then living and if during said two year period he has, in the opinion of my Trust-

ees, exhibited sufficient responsibility and stability to warrant distribution of a portion of my books to him, said books shall be divided by my Executor or Trustees between my son, EDWARD, and my granddaughter, FRANCESCA, in shares to be determined by my Trustees to be of approximate equal value [emphasis added]....
I recommend that my Trustees consider the possibility of selling such books as a collection at Parke-Bernet Galleries, Inc. in New York City.

Next there is this provision for a one-of-a-kind piano that Robinson owned:

I now own a certain piano which is unique in that it has been autographed by many of the great contemporary musicians. If I own said piano at the time of my death...I give and bequeath said piano to the UNIVER-SITY OF CALIFORNIA for the use of the School of Music at the Los Angeles campus of said University.

Finally, Robinson disposed of all his remaining tangible personal property as follows:

If I am survived by my wife, JANE, I give and bequeath all of my clothing, linens, pipes, souvenirs, mementos, and jewelry not otherwise disposed of hereunder, and similar personal effects to my said wife.... I request, but do not direct, that my wife give mementos from my personal effects to my brother, my nieces and nephews, and to such of our friends as she shall select, which mementos may have a particular sentimental meaning to the particular person selected as the recipient by my said wife.

I give and bequeath to my wife, JANE, for life, all my photographs, scripts, my self-portraits, records and

similar personal effects, pertaining to my career. Upon
the death of my said wife...I give and bequeath the
aforesaid property to the UNIVERSITY OF SOUTHERN
CALIFORNIA, a California corporation.

One has to wonder what wife Jane did with her husband's
pipe collection. Besides, people always thought of Robinson
as a cigar chomper.

During his life, Robinson was known to be generous with
friends and charity. The following provisions in his Will are
in line with that reputation.

BEQUESTS TO FRIENDS AND RELATIVES

The following gifts are small token gifts and do not in
any way measure my affection for the beneficiary. I give
and bequeath the following property to the following
persons:

A. To my friend, SAM JAFFE, the portrait of Sam Jaffe
painted by me.

G. To my niece, BEULAH GOLDBERG (also known as
BEAULA ROBINSON) the following amounts:

  1. If my said niece survives me, the sum of Five Thousand Dollars ($5,000).

  2. If my said niece survives me and she is unmarried
at the time of my death, I give and bequeath to her an
additional Two Thousand Five Hundred Dollars
($2,500.00) [Was a husband worth only $2,500 back
then?]

BEQUESTS TO CHARITY

I give and bequeath five percent (5%) of my net estate
...in equal shares to the following charitable organizations:

A. CITY COLLEGE OF NEW YORK, City of New York;

B. ACTORS FUND OF AMERICA (for the benefit of indigent actors);

C. MOTION PICTURE RELIEF FUND (for the care of residents of Motion Picture Country Home);

D. AMERICAN ACADEMY OF DRAMATIC ARTS, City of New York;

E. JEWISH COMMUNITY FOUNDATION OF THE JEWISH FEDERATION—COUNCIL OF LOS ANGELES;

F. N.A.A.C.P. LEGAL DEFENSE & EDUCATIONAL FUND.

Robinson's residuary estate was placed in trust for the benefit of his wife, son, and granddaughter. If none of them had survived him, which they all did, one-half of the estate was to be paid to the Motion Picture Relief Fund and the balance to Robinson relatives.

As befitting a product of the gangster era, Robinson's Will includes the following unusual "Contest Clause," which provides in part:

> Except as otherwise provided in this Will, I have intentionally and with full knowledge omitted to provide for my heirs. If any person other than my son, EDWARD, shall claim to be a child of mine or the descendant of a child of mine (other than my granddaughter, FRANCESCA, or her descendants), I direct my Executors to resist such claim; but if any court shall nevertheless determine that such person is a descendant of mine, I give to such person the sum of Ten Dollars ($10.00) and no more....

Any offspring of Little Caesar out there thinking about asserting a claim had only ten dollars to look forward to receiving.

Despite his long film career, Robinson never received an Academy Award for any of his performances. Robinson was to have received a special Oscar for his "outstanding contribution to motion pictures" at the Academy Awards ceremony scheduled for March of 1973. Unfortunately, the end for Rico came two months too soon.

/S/ Edward G. Robinson

WILL DATED: February 15, 1972

John Wayne

Date and Place of Birth	Date and Place of Death
May 26, 1907 Winterset, Iowa	June 11, 1979 U.C.L.A. Medical Center Los Angeles, California

Put Down Your Dukes

The paradigm of bygone American masculinity and virility, John Wayne swashbuckled his way though over two hundred films during his fifty-year film career. Finally, the man known as The Duke put down his guns and succumbed to multiple cancer of the lungs, abdomen, stomach, and intestines at the age of seventy-two.

Despite the all-American image, Wayne had been divorced twice, and as his Will indicates, his third marriage was on shaky ground. Wayne's Will begins:

> I am married to PILAR WAYNE, but she and I are separated, and for this reason I intentionally make no provision in this Will for her. I have seven (7) children whose names and respective birth dates are as follows: MICHAEL ANTHONY WAYNE, November 23, 1934; MARY ANTONIA LA CAVA, February 25, 1936; PATRICK JOHN WAYNE, July 15, 1939; MELINDA ANN MUNOZ, December 3, 1940, AISSA WAYNE, March 31, 1956; JOHN ETHAN WAYNE, February 22, 1962; and MARISA CARMELA WAYNE, February 22, 1966. The first four of the above-named children are the issue of my former marriage with Josephine A. Wayne; the last three of the above-named children are the issue of my

marriage with said Pilar. I and all of my said children
except Mary Antonia La Cava and Melinda Ann Munoz
are sometimes also known by the surname "Morrison."

Wayne's wife, Pilar Palette Wayne, was born in Peru. Wayne's
first two wives, Josephine Saenz and Esperanzo Bauer, were
also Latin Americans. It appears that one other part that
Wayne played offscreen was that of Latin lover.

Based on the provisions of the Will, it appears that the
Duke favored his eldest son, Michael. Michael is named as
co-executor of his father's Will, was appointed custodian of
any minor child's funds, and received a bequest of all Wayne's
preferred stock in his film company, Batjac Productions, Inc.
Wayne divides his tangible property, including any "motion
picture memorabilia or items whose value arises primarily
from their connection with my motion picture career," but
not including any "paintings, sculpture, American Indian ar-
tifacts, and other items having intrinsic merit and value,"
equally among his seven children. Those excluded "art objects" were to be donated to a charitable organization, selected
by the executors.

In the Will, Wayne makes a $10,000 bequest to a former
secretary and a $30,000 bequest to his current secretary.
Wayne establishes a trust fund for the benefit of his former
wife Josephine Morrison, which was to pay her the sum of
$3,000 per month, with the remainder to pass to her four
children after her death.

Living up to his reputation as a gunslinger, Wayne's Will
includes a final *in terrorem* clause stating:

If any beneficiary under this Will in any manner, directly or indirectly, contests or attacks this Will or any
of its provisions, any share or interest in my estate
given to that contesting beneficiary under this Will is
revoked and shall be disposed of in the same manner

provided herein as if that contesting beneficiary had
predeceased me without issue.

Now, that's true grit.

/S/ John Wayne

WILL DATED: October 5, 1978

William Holden

Date and Place of Birth	Date and Place of Death
April 17, 1918 O'Fallon, Illinois	November 16, 1981 535 Ocean Avenue (#5B) Santa Monica, California

Sunset on Ocean Avenue

Known in Hollywood circles as a dependable and normal family man for most of his career, actor William Holden made a Will and subsequent codicil that lived up to that reputation.

Holden's Will is devoted to family, friends, and the charitable causes that he believed in. The Will begins by stating:

> I am not now married. I was previously married to ARDIS HOLDEN, but our marriage was subsequently dissolved. We have two (2) children now living whose names are: PETER WESTFIELD HOLDEN, and SCOTT PORTER HOLDEN. I have no deceased children. My former wife, ARDIS HOLDEN, has a child by a former marriage, VIRGINIA BAYLOR. For purposes of this Will ... VIRGINIA BAYLOR shall be considered as my child and descendant, and her descendants shall be considered as my descendants.

Despite the divorce from his wife in the 1960s, Holden nonetheless provided for her and for her child from a previous marriage in his Will. Holden provided for his former wife by making her a beneficiary of the trust holding his residuary

51

estate, which provided that income was to be paid to Holden's descendants, former wife, and mother. In a codicil to the Will, Holden added his niece, the child of Holden's deceased brother, as a beneficiary of his estate. Now, that is a family man.

But the plot gets thicker. Holden also made a $250,000 bequest to actress Stephanie Powers, who was his frequent companion in his later years. There were also $50,000 bequests to a woman residing in Switzerland, where Holden spent several years, and to a woman who lived in Newport Beach, California. Furthermore, the Will forgives any debts owed to Holden or his estate by anyone from a group of eleven people named in the Will, including Miss Powers.

During the middle of his career, Holden took seven years off from filmmaking and moved abroad to Switzerland, Hong Kong, and Kenya, Africa. During that period, Holden became a wildlife conservationist and was the founder of the Mount Kenya Safari Club. In his Will, Holden provides that if he owned any property or business interests in the Republic of Kenya in Africa, that property should be given to a charity "which is interested in the preservation of wild life and the environment and, if at all possible, has ties to or interests in Africa and, more specifically, the Republic of Kenya." At the same time, Holden bequeathed his extensive gun collection in equal shares to his two sons, Peter and Scott. His two sons also received $75,000 bequests and were beneficiaries of the residuary trust.

Holden named the Title Insurance and Trust Company of Los Angeles, California, as the executor of his Will and as trustee of the trust.

At the age of sixty-three, William Holden was found dead in his seaside apartment in Santa Monica, California. According to the police report, Holden had died of natural causes two or three days prior to being found by the manager of the apartment building. Though his permanent home was in Palm

Springs, California, and he spent time on his land in Kenya, the sun set on the golden boy while alone in an apartment on Ocean Avenue overlooking the Pacific Ocean.

/S/ *William F. Holden*

WILL DATED: April 6, 1979
CODICIL DATED: August 24, 1979
Signed in Los Angeles, California

Henry Fonda

Date and Place of Birth	Date and Place of Death
May 16, 1905 Grand Island, Nebraska	August 12, 1982 Cedars-Sinai Medical Center Los Angeles, California

Beyond Golden Pond

One of America's most beloved actors, Henry Fonda starred in more than one hundred films and theatrical productions, but an Academy Award for Best Actor eluded Fonda until his last film, *On Golden Pond*, which Mr. Fonda made shortly before his death with his daughter, Jane, and costar Katharine Hepburn. Henry Fonda was married to five women during his life. His first marriage, to actress Margaret Sullavan, ended in divorce in 1933. His second wife, Frances Seymour Brokaw, was the mother of Jane and Peter. Reportedly, she killed herself in a sanitarium in 1950. During his third marriage, to Susan Blanchard, Fonda adopted a daughter, Amy. That marriage ended in divorce. So did Fonda's fourth marriage, to Contessa Afdera Franchetti. At the time of his death, Fonda was involved in his fifth marriage, to Shirlee Mae Adams. The first article of Fonda's Will states:

> I declare that I am married to Shirlee Adams Fonda, and that we have no issue. I further declare that I have three children by previous marriages: My daughters Jane Fonda Hayden and Amy Fonda Fishman, and my son Peter Henry Fonda.

The Will that is excerpted herein was signed about a year and a half before Fonda died. The codicil, which was signed

54

six months later, shows a significant change of mind by Fonda regarding who should handle his affairs after his death.

In his Will, Fonda appoints wife Shirlee, son Peter, and his attorney as executors of his Will. In the codicil to his Will Fonda removes son Peter as an executor and substitutes a new attorney, and wife Shirlee stays in place.

The three-page Will includes a $200,000 bequest to Fonda's daughter Amy, if she survived him by ninety days, which she did. There are no bequests for daughter Jane or son Peter in the Will, and about that Fonda states:

> I am providing primarily for my wife Shirlee and my daughter Amy because they are dependent upon me for their support. I have made no provision in this Will for Jane or Peter, or for their families, solely because in my opinion they are financially independent, and my decision is not in any sense a measure of my deep affection for them.

With that said, Fonda's Will also includes an *in terrorem* clause to inhibit any possible attacks or objections to the Will. However, it was no secret that Fonda's relations with his politically activist daughter Jane and *Easy Rider* son Peter were known to be occasionally stormy.

Under the Will, Fonda leaves all his "personal effects, clothing and automobiles . . . furniture, furnishings and objects of art" and his entire residuary estate to his wife, Shirlee. If Shirlee did not survive him, then his entire residuary estate was left

> to the Omaha Community Playhouse, at Omaha, Nebraska, to be used for such capital improvements, and for the maintenance and operation thereof, as the governing body of said Playhouse deems proper, this gift to be known as "The Henry and Shirlee Fonda Bequest."

Fonda, who was born near Omaha, was a generous supporter of its local playhouse during his lifetime.

Known as an honest and self-effacing man with a great ability to act, Henry Fonda did not want a grandiose or large funeral. On that question, the Will simply states:

> It is my wish that there be no funeral or memorial service at the time of my death, and that my remains be promptly cremated and disposed of without ceremony of any kind.

A few months after winning his first Oscar for his heart-warming performance in *On Golden Pond*, Henry Fonda went beyond Golden Pond and died from a weak heart at the age of seventy-seven. At Fonda's bedside when he died were wife Shirlee, daughters Jane and Amy, and son Peter, but all of America mourned the loss of one of the most beloved actors of our time.

/S/ Henry Fonda

WILL DATED: January 22, 1981
CODICIL DATED: July 9, 1981

Rock Hudson

Date and Place of Birth	Date and Place of Death
November 17, 1925 Winnetka, Illinois	October 2, 1985 9402 Beverly Crescent Drive Beverly Hills, California

Bad Day at Castle Rock

That one of the silver screen's most rugged, handsome "lady-killers" died of acquired immune deficiency syndrome (AIDS) allegedly stemming from his homosexual activities was one of the great ironies of the 1980s. Hudson's AIDS-related death resulted in a widely reported lawsuit against his estate brought by Rock's former lover Marc Christian. Mr. Christian claimed he had suffered serious injury by not being informed of Hudson's contagious medical condition. And a Los Angeles jury agreed, awarding Mr. Christian millions of dollars in damages against Hudson's estate.

Hudson, who was named Roy Scherer, Jr., at birth and subsequently took the surname of his stepfather, Wallace Fitzgerald, changed his name to the more masculine-sounding "Rock Hudson" at the suggestion of his agent around 1947.

Hudson was married for three years during the 1950s to his agent's secretary, Phyllis Gates. Whether this marriage was for the sake of appearances or true love or a combination of both, we will never know for sure, but in any case, the gate closed on their marriage in 1958. After that, Hudson's homosexual tendencies were a well-kept Hollywood secret until word leaked to the public shortly before Hudson's death. Toward the end of his life, Hudson was less secretive about his homosexuality and often had homosexual romps around his Beverly Hills home known as The Castle. It was in his bedroom in The Castle that Hudson finally stopped rocking, dying in his sleep.

Since the early 1970s Hudson was intimately involved with Tom Clark, who for many years was Hudson's live-in lover and handled Hudson's personal affairs. For Tom Clark, the fourth article of Hudson's 1981 Will provides the following:

> I give to TOM H. CLARK all of my automobiles, household furniture and furnishings, clothing, art objects, jewelry, motion picture equipment, my collection of motion picture films, cassettes and all other tangible personal property and personal effects of mine. TOM H. CLARK may retain for himself those items that he would like to as a memento and may distribute the other items among such other friends of mine whom he may select and the persons and organizations named in the revocable trust created by me, dated April 3, 1974 and all amendments thereto made prior to my death which TOM H. CLARK deems would be appropriate for them to have. The balance of such items may be given to such charitable organizations which TOM H. CLARK deems it would be appropriate for them to have....

This provision affords Clark great discretion in the disposition of Hudson's tangible property, which was quite substantial. Unfortunately for Clark, in a codicil that Hudson signed at his New York lawyers' offices on August 23, 1984, Hudson bluntly revokes that gift with the following:

> I hereby delete in its entirety Article FOURTH of my said Last Will and Testament. I purposely make no provision for the benefit of TOM H. CLARK.

It appears that Clark had fallen from Rock's grace, but no one was named to take his place.

According to his Will, Hudson's entire residuary estate was to be "poured over" into the revocable trust created in 1974. The terms of that trust are private and did not have to be filed with the court. Hudson's business manager and accountant, Wallace Sheft, was named as the executor of the Will and was trustee of the 1974 trust.

Hudson's Will included a "One Dollar ($1.00)" *in terrorem* clause and the statement that "except as otherwise provided in this Will, I have intentionally and with full knowledge, and not by accident or mistake, omitted to provide herein for my heirs living at the time of my death."

Despite the *in terrorem* clause young Christian was not deterred from making a claim against the estate. Because Christian was not mentioned in the Will and had no family relationship with Hudson, he did not contest the Will, but instead made a claim for damages against Hudson's estate for the decedent's failure to disclose his fatal illness to his former lover. Christian had nothing to lose, other than his life.

Finally, Hudson's Will, which he had signed before being diagnosed with AIDS, provided for the following disposition of his remains: "I request that I be cremated and that my cremated remains be scattered in the channel between Wilmington and Catalina Island." It has been reported that the cut-out Clark insisted on being the only one to hold the urn with Rock's remains and to scatter Rock's ashes in his last channel.

/S/ *Roy H. Fitzgerald*

WILL DATED: August 18, 1981
CODICIL DATED: August 23, 1984
Signed at 410 Park Avenue, New York, New York

Cary Grant

Date and Place of Birth	Date and Place of Death
January 18, 1904 Bristol, England	November 29, 1986 Davenport, Iowa

He Was No Angel

Born to a working-class family in the English port city of Bristol and named Archibald Alexander Leach, film star Cary Grant had a suave and elegant manner that drove women mad. Based on his own marital history, it appears that at least four women drove Grant mad; he was divorced four times.

Mr. Grant's first wife was actress Virginia Cherrill. His second wife was the heiress Barbara Hutton. His third wife was another actress, Betsy Drake. His fourth wife was the actress Dyan Cannon, with whom Grant had his beloved daughter, Jennifer. At the time of his death, Grant was married to his fifth wife, Barbara Harris.

To avoid any possible confusion, Grant's 1984 Will describes the two women most important to him as follows:

I am married to BARBARA HARRIS GRANT; and all references in this Will to "my wife" are to her.

I declare that I have had and now have only one child, a daughter, JENNIFER GRANT, born February 27, 1966. Said JENNIFER GRANT was born of my marriage to DYAN GRANT [presently known as DYAN CANNON], which marriage was dissolved by a final judgement of divorce dated March 21, 1969. All references in this Will to "my daughter" are to said JENNIFER GRANT.

In his Will, Grant divides his residuary estate equally between his said wife and in trust for his daughter until she reached age thirty-five. At the time of Grant's death, Jennifer was twenty years old. In addition, he gave to his wife his residence at 9966 Beverly Grove Drive in Los Angeles, California, and all his "household furniture, furnishings, appliances, works of art of all kinds, silver and silverware, automobiles and other tangible items," excluding his personal effects. To dispose of his personal effects. Grant provided the following:

> I give and bequeath all of my wearing apparel, ornaments and jewelry ... to STANLEY E. FOX, with the understanding that although this bequest to him is absolute, and not impressed with any trust, it is nevertheless my wish and desire that he shall distribute certain of my tangible effects as I may at any time hereafter designate ... to any of the following persons: (1) my wife, BARBARA HARRIS GRANT; (2) my daughter, JENNIFER; (3) my friends, MRS. LESLEY HARRIS, BETSY DRAKE GRANT, IRENE SELZNICK, MARGE EVERETT, NORMAN ZEILER, CHARLES RICH, KIRK KERKORIAN, FRANK SINATRA, RODERICK MANN, STANLEY DONEN, WILLIE LEE WATSON, and STANLEY E. FOX; and (4) such other of my friends and relatives whom I may mention to STANLEY E. FOX from time to time ... it is my hope that he shall endeavor to make distribution of said items in a manner satisfactory and fair to all concerned.

It appears that Grant was not chicken about letting Fox, who was Grant's friend and business adviser, make some important decisions after he had departed.

Besides taking care of his wife and daughter, Grant was also generous with several employees and friends. To one employee he bequeathed $100,000 and to another $25,000. For the Motion Picture Relief Fund, Inc., Grant left the sum of $50,000. He bequeathed the Variety Club International and the John Tracy Clinic in Los Angeles the sum of $25,000 each.

The final article of Grant's Will states, "I desire that my remains be cremated, and that there be no formal services to note my passing." Grant died suddenly from a stroke at the age of eighty-two before appearing at a fund-raising event in Davenport, Iowa. It would be hard to imagine that the death of acting great Cary Grant could pass without notice, as he had requested in his Will.

/S/ Cary Grant

WILL DATED: November 26, 1984
Signed at Beverly Hills, California

THE MUSIC MEN

Dead Beats

The Music Man	Date of Death
Cole Porter Everything Goes	October 15, 1964
Jim Morrison "This Is the End, Beautiful Friend"	July 3, 1971
Elvis Presley The King Is Dead	August 16, 1977
Bing Crosby The Nineteenth Hole	October 14, 1977
John Lennon Strawberry Fields Forever	December 8, 1980
Count Basie Out for the Count	April 26, 1984
Ricky Nelson "The Miss Adventures of Ricky Nelson"	December 31, 1985

Vladimir Horowitz

November 5, 1989

High Strung

Cole Porter

Date and Place of Birth	Date and Place of Death
June 9, 1892	October 15, 1964
Peru, Indiana	Santa Monica Hospital
	Santa Monica, California

Everything Goes

Songwriter Cole Porter composed the lyrics and music to scores of the most memorable songs the world would ever hear. Porter's songs were known for lyrics that were sophisticated and witty and include such classics as "Anything Goes," "I Get a Kick out of You," and the titillating "Let's Do It."

In the summer of 1937, when he was forty-five years old and at the height of his success, Porter was in a horseback-riding accident that broke both his legs, seriously injured his central nervous system, and changed his outlook on life—from a wheelchair. After his wife of thirty-five years, the former Linda Lee Thomas, died in 1954, and Porter's right leg was amputated in 1958, Porter became even more reclusive, spending most of his time holed up in his memorabilia-filled apartment at New York's Waldorf-Astoria.

Cole Porter's lengthy and detailed Will is as much a product of his fascinating life and collections (both of objects and friends) as the drafting techniques of the fancy Park Avenue law firm that prepared it. Despite the intricate legalese, Cole Porter's own style and priorities nonetheless shine through.

The first section of Porter's Will indicates his desire to return to the soil of his birthplace in Peru, Indiana, and Porter's last personal requests of a religious nature.

65

I DIRECT my Executors to arrange for my burial in Peru, Indiana. I FURTHER DIRECT my Executors to arrange for no funeral or memorial service, but only for a private burial service to be conducted by the Pastor of the First Baptist Church of Peru, in the presence of my relatives and dear friends. At such service I request said Pastor to read the following quotation from the Bible:

"I am the resurrection and the life;
he that believeth in me, though he were
dead, yet shall he live; And whosoever
liveth and believeth in me shall never die,"

and to follow such quotation with The Lord's Prayer. I request that the foregoing be substantially the entire burial service, and that neither said Pastor nor anyone else deliver any memorial address whatsoever. I particularly direct that there be no service of any kind for me in New York City.

Following the burial instructions, the Will proceeds to divide Porter's varied estate among educational and charitable institutions, friends, and employees, but primarily among Porter's relatives.

To Williams College, Porter gave the 350-acre estate, known as Buxton Hill, that he owned in Williamstown, Massachusetts. He gave all the pianos in his New York apartment to The Juilliard School of Music and all his cigarette cases and scrapbooks to the Museum of Modern Art. Porter divides his papers and books among Williams College, Yale University, and the University of California at Los Angeles. Finally, he bequeathed all his clothing to the Salvation Army.

The following are some of the more unusual and provocative personal bequests made in Porter's Will:

I GIVE AND BEQUEATH to each of the following persons who shall survive me the article or articles of tangible personal property, which I shall own at my death, set forth below opposite the name of such person:

C. The DUKE OF VERDURA, the Justiani-Capo de Monte china service and my Ginori dessert plates...

E. MRS. WILLIAM (EDITH) GOETZ, the Cambodian head sculpture, which is now located in my apartment in New York, New York, and the small (9" x 12") water color painting of a seashore scene framed in a gilt frame.

F. EDGAR M. (MONTY) WOOLLEY, the star sapphire cuff links, waistcoat buttons and studs for shirt.

G. DOUGLAS FAIRBANKS, JR., the diamond dress stud.

H. BARON NICOLAS DE GUNZBURG, the Russian ikon, which is now located in my apartment in New York, New York; the sculpture of an Egyptian woman's head, which is now located in my cottage on my Buxton Hill Realty; and the book by Paul Muratoff, which was published by A La Vielle Russie and which is entitled "Thirty-Five Russian Primitives."

I. MISS AVA ASTAIRE, the aquamarine and ruby necklace which formerly belonged to my beloved wife, Linda Porter.

All the rest of his tangible property, "including, without limitation, my automobiles, silver, household furniture furnishings and utensils, rugs, carpets, tapestries, bric-a-brac, sculpture, paintings, china, glassware, objects of art, jewelry and personal effects," Porter left to his cousin, Jules Omar Cole, or if he did not survive, to Jules's son, James Omar Cole. One has to wonder about the meaning of "bric-a-brac" within that comprehensive context. The distinction between "carpets" and "rugs" for this purpose might also be a bit of legal overkill. How about "floor coverings of any kind"? I know, more letters.

Porter also made cash bequests ranging from $1,000 to

$10,000 to certain friends and employees. The bulk of Porter's wealthy estate and continuing royalty payments is held by a trust for the benefit of Porter family relatives. Over twenty-five years after Porter's death, his estate is generating income in excess of $3 million per year. With that kind of money, anything goes.

/S/ *Cole Porter*

WILL DATED: November 28, 1962

Jim Morrison

Date and Place of Birth	Date and Place of Death
December 8, 1943	July 3, 1971
Melbourne, Florida	Paris, France

"This Is the End, Beautiful Friend"

When rock superstar Jim Morrison died at the age of twenty-seven in a bathtub in Paris, he left a lyrical legacy that is etched into the consciousness of a generation. As the incendiary lead singer for the sixties rock group The Doors, Morrison helped light the flames and fan the fires of that decade. One of The Doors' first and best-known songs was "Light My Fire," which became an anthem for the flower children of the sixties. Another song, performed particularly graphically by Morrison, was "The End," in which the protagonist in the song has an Oedipal encounter with his mother and ends up murdering both of his parents. Strange days, indeed.

Morrison signed his one-page Will in Beverly Hills, California, in the office of his lawyer, Max Fink. Fink is named a co-executor, together with Morrison's then girlfriend and future wife, Pamela S. Courson. The Will begins as follows:

I, JAMES D. MORRISON, being of sound and disposing mind, memory and understanding, and after consideration for all persons, the objects of my bounty, and with full knowledge of the nature and extent of my assets,

do hereby make, publish and declare this my Last Will
and Testament, as follows:

FIRST: I declare that I am a resident of Los Angeles
County, California; that I am unmarried and have no
children.

To his then girlfriend, Pamela S. Courson, Morrison left
"each and every thing of value of which I may die possessed,
including real property, personal property and mixed properties," or in other words, his entire estate. If Pamela had not
survived Morrison for three months after his death, then the
estate was to be left to Morrison's brother, Andrew Morrison
of Monterey, California, and to his sister, Anne R. Morrison
of Coronado Beach, California, "to share and share alike."
Neither of Morrison's parents, George S. Morrison and Clara
Morrison, were mentioned in his Will. During his lifetime,
Morrison had often stated that both his parents were dead.
In fact, they both survived their prodigal son.

Morrison's girlfriend, Pamela Courson, married Morrison
after he had signed his Will. She survived her husband by
the requisite three-month period, but died about three years
later on April 25, 1974. Pamela Courson Morrison's father,
Columbus B. Courson, succeeded his daughter as administrator of Jim Morrison's estate and as its sole beneficiary. One
has to wonder whether Mr. Columbus Courson had approved
of the lifestyle and antics of his daughter's boyfriend and then
husband. As might be expected, attorney Max Fink filed all
the legal documents required.

After his death in Paris, Morrison was buried in the famous
Parisian cemetery Père la Chaise. He was buried near some
of the symbolist and surrealist poets whose writings had in-
spired his own poetry (with the help of large quantities of a
variety of intoxicants). Dead before he was even close to thirty,
Jim Morrison left a rock-and-roll legacy of fire and passion
that will not be forgotten. As Morrison himself once

sang, "I'll tell you this/ No eternal reward will forgive us now for wasting the dawn." Jim Morrison did not waste his dawns, his dawns wasted him.

/S/ *James D. Morrison*

WILL DATED: February 12, 1969

Elvis Presley

Date and Place of Birth	Date and Place of Death
January 8, 1935 Tupelo, Mississippi	August 16, 1977 Baptist Memorial Hospital Memphis, Tennessee

The King Is Dead

The undisputed King of Rock and Roll, Elvis Presley, died at the age of forty-two shortly after he was found unconscious in his bedroom at his home in Memphis called Graceland. The cause of death was officially termed a "cardiac arrhythmia," which may have been a result of Presley's excess weight and the pills he took to suppress his appetite. Presley reportedly had an appetite for Cadillacs, "Girls, Girls, Girls," drugs, and liquor, as well as food.

On May 1, 1967, Presley married Priscilla Beaulieu, who was an Air Force brat he had met during his own Army stint. On February 1, 1968, a daughter they named Lisa Marie was born. In 1973, Elvis and Priscilla Presley were divorced.

When Presley died about five months after signing his Will, he was survived by his nine-year-old daughter, Lisa Marie, his father, Vernon, and his grandmother, Minnie Mae Presley. Presley's 1977 Will provides primarily for these three people. A trust of the entire residuary estate is established for their benefit, and for any other Presley relatives "who in the absolute discretion of my Trustee are in need of emergency assistance for any of the above mentioned purposes," which included "health, education, support, comfortable maintenance and welfare."

Presley appointed his father, Vernon E. Presley, as the executor of the Will and as trustee. Pop Presley is given broad discretion over the affairs of the estate. For example, there is the following "Item" in the Will concerning Elvis's "trophies":

Instructions Concerning Personal Property: Enjoyment in Specie

I anticipate that included as a part of my property and estate at the time of my death will be tangible personal property of various kinds, characters and values, including trophies and other items accumulated by me during my professional career. I hereby specifically instruct all concerned that my Executor, herein appointed, shall have complete freedom and discretion as to disposal of any and all such property so long as he shall act in good faith and in the best interest of my estate and my beneficiaries, and his discretion so exercised shall not be subject to question by anyone whomsoever.

Presley's Will was prepared by local Tennessee attorneys. At one point in the Will, Elvis gets technical when he states, "Having in mind the rule against perpetuities, I direct that (notwithstanding anything contained to the contrary in this Last Will and Testament) . . ." It is a good thing that Presley's attorneys did not write his songs.

The Will, which was apparently prepared in 1976 but not signed until 1977, concludes with the following:

IN WITNESS WHEREOF, I, the said ELVIS A. PRESLEY, do hereunto set my hand and seal in the presence of two (2) competent witnesses, and in their presence do

publish and declare this instrument to be my Last Will
and Testament, this ___3___ day of ___March___, ~~1976~~
                                                    1977

/S/ Elvis A. Presley

That witness clause would have been fine, except there were,
in fact, three witnesses to Presley's Will. The Will had been
prepared for the signatures of only two witnesses, but it appears that an extra Presley fan slipped in there when he was
signing.

Elvis's father, Vernon Presley, died in 1979. In 1989, the
estate was terminated, with all the property, including Graceland, held in trust for the benefit of Presley's then twenty-
one-year-old daughter, Lisa Marie, until she reaches age
twenty-five. At twenty-five, Lisa Marie Presley will inherit a
fortune, if not fame, and is probably not lonesome tonight.

WILL DATED: March 3, 1977
Will signed in Memphis, Tennessee

Bing Crosby

Date and Place of Birth	Date and Place of Death
May 2, 1904 Tacoma, Washington	October 14, 1977 La Moraleja Golf Club Madrid, Spain

The Nineteenth Hole

Bing Crosby had a melodious singing voice and easygoing manner that made him one of America's most beloved entertainers for over five decades. However, it was revealed in a 1983 book by son Gary Crosby called *Going My Own Way* that the publicly easygoing Bing was a strict disciplinarian at home with his children.

Crosby was named Harry Lillis Crosby at his birth in Tacoma, Washington. The nickname Bing came early, and it stuck. In 1930 Bing married Wilma Winifred Wyatt, who was a film star known professionally as Dixie Lee. They had four sons before Dixie Lee Crosby died in 1952. In 1957, Crosby married a woman less than half his age, Kathryn Grant, a twenty-three-year old actress from Texas. They had three children—Harry Lillis Crosby 3d, Nathaniel Patrick Crosby, and Mary Frances Crosby. Bing's June 1977 Will describes his family as follows:

I am married to KATHRYN GRANT CROSBY, who in this Will is referred to as "my Wife." I have the following children:

GARY EVAN CROSBY;

PHILIP LANG CROSBY;

DENNIS MICHAEL CROSBY;

LINDSAY HARRY CROSBY;
HARRY LILLIS CROSBY, III;
MARY FRANCES CROSBY; and
NATHANIEL PATRICK CROSBY.

In his Will Crosby makes the following cash bequests to his wife, certain other family relatives (but not his children), and three charities in Spokane, Washington, where Crosby had studied law at Gonzaga University before dropping out to pursue his interest in music:

I make the following cash gifts:
(a) To my Wife, KATHRYN GRANT CROSBY, $150,000.
(b) To my niece, CAROLYN MILLER, $15,000.
(c) To my niece, MARILYN McLACHLAN, $15,000.
(d) To my sister, MARY ROSE POOL, $20,000.
(e) To my niece, CATHERINE CROSBY, the daughter of my brother, TED, $10,000.
(f) To my niece, MARY SUE SHANNON, $10,000.

(1) To SAINT ALOYSIUS CHURCH, Spokane, Washington, $5,000.
(m) To GONZAGA UNIVERSITY, Spokane, Washington, $50,000.
(n) To GONZAGA HIGH SCHOOL, Spokane, Washington, $50,000.

In addition, Crosby gave all his personal property including "my automobiles, jewelry, silverware, books, paintings, works of art, household furniture and furnishings, clothing, and other personal effects" to his wife, Kathryn, if she survived. If she did not survive him, that property was to pass as part of Crosby's residuary estate.

According to his Will, Crosby's residuary estate is given to the Harry L. Crosby Trust, which he established on the same day he signed his Will. The provisions of that trust are private, but it is telling that publicly easygoing Bing included a very comprehensive *in terrorem* clause in his Will that refers to Crosby's children as follows.

Provision Against Contest.

Except as otherwise provided in this Will and the trust referred to in CLAUSE EIGHTH I have intentionally and with full knowledge omitted to provide for my heirs, and I have specifically failed to provide for any child of mine whether mentioned in this Will or in said trust or otherwise....

Finally, it is noteworthy that the funeral instructions in his Will show Crosby to be a self-effacing and religious person:

I direct that my funeral services be conducted in a Catholic church; that they be completely private with attendance limited to my wife and the above mentioned children; that a low mass [emphasis added] be said and that no memorial service of any kind be held. I further direct that insofar as possible services be held without any publicity, other than that which my family permits after my burial, which shall be in a Catholic cemetery.

Crosby collapsed of a heart attack on a golf course in Spain after having completed a very respectable eighteen holes of golf. Shortly after learning of her husband's death, Kathryn Crosby was quoted at a news conference as saying, "I can't think of any better way for a golfer who sings for a living to finish the round."

/S/ *Harry L. Crosby*

WILL DATED: June 27, 1977
Will signed at Los Angeles, California

John Lennon

Date and Place of Birth	Date and Place of Death
October 9, 1940 Liverpool, England	December 8, 1980 The Dakota, 1 West 72nd Street New York, New York

Strawberry Fields Forever

Senselessly murdered by a deranged drifter at the street entrance to his home in New York City, Beatle John Lennon left a legacy of music, lyrics, and wit that changed the world. The Beatles' rise from tough-club obscurity to being the objects of "Beatlemania" sweeping the world was quite meteoric and could have turned calmer heads. And Lennon was no calm head to begin with. His experimentations with a variety of mind-altering techniques including meditation, hallucinogenic drugs, cannabis, heroin, and yoga have all widely been reported and only add to the mystical aura surrounding Lennon.

Lennon's devotion to his Japanese-born wife, Yoko Ono, has been called one cause of the breakup of the Beatles in 1970. In that same year, Lennon dedicated a solo album entitled *Plastic Ono Band* to Yoko. In that album, Lennon describes his relationship with God and Yoko as follows: "God is a concept by which we measure our pain." He then lists those things he does not believe in: magic, I-Ching, Bible, tarot, Hitler, Jesus, Kennedy, Buddha, mantra, Gita, yoga, kings, Elvis, Zimmerman, or Beatles. "I just believe in me, Yoko and me, and that's reality."

The November 1979 Will that Lennon signed is unusually vague and unstructured for a person with the enormous wealth and copyright considerations that Lennon would have had. Yoko is the only named beneficiary. She received one-half of Lennon's enormous estate outright, and for the other half, the Will states:

> I give, devise and bequeath all the rest, residue and remainder of my estate, wheresoever situate, to the Trustees under a Trust Agreement dated November 12, 1979, which I signed with my wife, YOKO ONO, and ELI GARBER as Trustees...

After John's death, Yoko was in complete control of John's wealth.

As a result of the sheer volume of Beatles albums sold and royalties received for his compositions, Lennon was a very wealthy man. The income from principal alone was a significant sum. Yoko Ono was known to be the business manager in the family, with John assuming the role of "house husband" and primarily rearing his son Sean, who was around five years old when his father was killed.

Without knowing the provisions of the private trust referred to in the Will, we can only wonder whether Lennon made any provisions for his beloved son Sean, older son Julian from his first marriage to Cynthia Powers, or any of the other people in Lennon's life.

As one would expect, the Will contains the following provision regarding Lennon's designation of executor:

> I hereby nominate, constitute and appoint my beloved wife YOKO ONO, to act as the Executor of this my Last Will and Testament. In the event that my beloved wife YOKO ONO shall predecease me or chooses not to act for any reason, I nominate and appoint ELI GARBER, DAVID WARMFLASH and CHARLES PETTIT, in the order named, to act in her place and stead.

Garber was the Lennons' accountant and Warmflash was both Lennons' attorney and had prepared John's Will.

It is somewhat unusual and totally unnecessary for a husband to appoint his wife as the guardian of their children, but that is exactly what Lennon did in the following clause in his Will:

> I nominate, constitute and appoint my wife YOKO ONO, as the Gurdian [*sic*] of the person and property of any children of the marriage who may survive me. In the event that she predeceases me, or for any reason she chooses not to act in that capacity, I nominate, constitute and appoint SAM GREEN to act in her place and stead.

Sam Green was an intimate employee of the Lennons who had a good rapport with Sean and was obviously trusted by John.

At the end of the Will, there is an unusual *in terrorem* clause that reads as follows:

> If any legatee or beneficiary under this Will or the trust agreement between myself as Grantor and YOKO ONO LENNON and ELI GARBER as Trustees, dated November 12, 1979 shall interpose objections to the probate of this Will, or institute or prosecute or be in any way interested or instrumental in the institution or prosecution of any action or proceeding for the purpose of setting aside or invalidating this Will, then and in each such case, I direct that such legatee or beneficiary shall receive nothing whatsoever under this Will or the aforementioned Trust.

This is certainly a strange provision to include because the only direct beneficiary in the Will was Yoko Ono, and it would be patently clear that she would have no objection to the Will.

Lennon's unusually short Will concludes as follows:

IN WITNESS WHEREOF, I have subscribed and sealed and do publish and declare these presents as and for my Last Will and Testament, this 12th day of November, 1979.

/S/ J Lennon

THE FOREGOING INSTRUMENT consisting of four (4) typewritten pages, including this page, was on the 12th day of November, 1979, signed, sealed, published and declared by JOHN WINSTON ONO LENNON, the Testator therein named, as and for his Last Will and Testament, in the present [*sic*] of us, who at his request, and in his presence, and in the presence of each other, have hereunto set our names as witnesses.

That sounds like a lot of presents, considering no one but Yoko got anything under the Will.

It is sadly ironic that Lennon signed this Will at the Dakota, "One West 72nd Street, New York, New York," the same address and only a few hundred feet from the spot where he was fatally shot on a cold December night returning from the recording studio. In the 1970s, Lennon had vigorously resisted deportation from the United States and won a legal victory in 1976 that allowed him to remain at his home in New York.

The preamble to Lennon's Will reads, "I, JOHN WINSTON ONO LENNON, a resident of the County of New York, State of New York, which I declare to be my domicile..." The lad from Liverpool was enjoying living in New York, but tragically, it was on the mean streets of New York where John Lennon fought to remain that he died a tragic and untimely death.

One of the ways in which Yoko Ono commemorated her husband's death was by donating funds to New York City to replant and relandscape a section of Central Park near the Lennons' apartment and naming it Strawberry Fields, "where nothing is real." Unfortunately for Lennon, and the world, the streets of New York were all too real.

/S/ John Lennon

WILL DATED: November 12, 1979

Count Basie

Date and Place of Birth

August 21, 1904
Red Bank, New Jersey

Date and Place of Death

April 26, 1984
Doctors' Hospital
Hollywood, Florida

Out for the Count

A king of swing, a jazz great, and one of the leading bandleaders of the century, William Basie was an only son born into a poor black family in New Jersey. Despite racial barriers, by his incredible musical talents, charm, and wit, young William joined the ranks of other musical nobility such as "Duke" Ellington and "Earl" Hines and was dubbed "Count" early in his career.

When he died of the bigger C (cancer) at the age of seventy-nine, Basie was living in Freeport in the Grand Bahamas. Basie's wife, Catherine, had died in 1983, and he was survived by his only daughter, Diane Basie, also of Freeport. In his Will, Basie places his entire estate in trust for his daughter's benefit. If she had not survived, then the Basie estate was to be divided three ways. As the Will states:

> I give, bequeath and devise all the rest, residue and remainder of my property ... to the following individuals, who are then surviving, in equal shares: LAMONT GILMORE, ROSEMARIE MATTHEWS, and AARON WOODWARD, all of whom I have sometimes affectionately referred to as my children, although none are my natural children nor legally adopted by me. [emphasis added]

Although his permanent home was in the Grand Bahamas, Basie requests under the first article of his Will that he be cremated and "my ashes buried in Pine Lawn Mausoleum, located in Farmingdale, Long Island." When the Count finally laid down his baton, he apparently felt more comfortable in northern soil than in a tropical paradise.

/S/ *William J. Basie*

WILL DATED: February 13, 1984

Ricky Nelson

Date and Place of Birth	Date and Place of Death
May 8, 1940 Teaneck, New Jersey	December 31, 1985 De Kalb, Texas

"The Miss Adventures of Ricky Nelson"

*E*ric ("Ricky") Hilliard Nelson was the younger son of Ozzie and Harriet Nelson of Teaneck, New Jersey. During the 1940s, 1950s, and 1960s, the Nelson family entertained in living rooms all across America until "The Adventures of Ozzie and Harriet" ended in 1966. After that, Ricky Nelson continued a successful career in music.

It was on the way to a New Year's Eve concert when Nelson's own DC-3 airplane crashed and burned in De Kalb, Texas, approximately thirty-five miles from Texarkana, Texas. Aboard the plane with Ricky was his twenty-seven-year-old fiancée, Helen Blair, who also died in the crash together with five others. Nelson signed this Will less than five months before his death.

Nelson's Will does not mince any words when describing his marital history and family relationships.

SECOND: I hereby declare that I am not married at this time and was divorced from KRISTIN NELSON in 1982 and specifically and intentionally fail to provide for her herein.

THIRD: I hereby declare that I have four children of said aforementioned marriage, specifically: TRACY NELSON, GUNNAR NELSON, MATTHEW NELSON and SAM NELSON. I hereby give, devise and bequeath all the rest, residue and remainder of my estate...to said four beloved children, in equal shares, share and share alike....

It gets rougher as under the eighth article of the Will, Nelson expressly disinherits a named child: "I specifically fail to provide herein for a minor, ERIC CREWE as I dispute the paternity of said minor child."

Next the Will makes the following two statements about the two most important women in Nelson's life at that time:

SEVENTH: I have specifically failed to provide for my mother HARRIET NELSON as she is well taken-care of and comfortable at this time.

NINTH: I specifically fail to provide herein for HELEN BLAIR as that is our wishes.

The fact that Nelson failed to provide in his Will for his fiancée, Helen Blair, obviously did not make any difference, as she died with him in the plane crash.

Nelson named his brother, David Nelson, as the executor of his Will. Ricky's personal manager, Greg McDonald, is named as a successor executor and also given the following authority:

I further direct that my personal manager and good friend, GREG McDONALD retain full control over the management of all my show business properties, past present and future including all publishing rights and decisions of MATRA-GUN/NELSON MUSIC. He shall also have full power and control to make all creative decisions for the use of my name, likeness and biography in perpetuity. In compensation for his services, GREG McDONALD shall be paid the usual fee of 15% of all gross revenues from said ventures. The remaining funds generated therefrom shall be divided evenly between my four children as hereinbefore provided. The revenues from my family television show, "The Adventures of Ozzie and Harriet" are specifically excluded from this paragraph, as to McDonald.

Nelson's Will also includes the following patently incorrect *in terrorem* clause:

I have intentionally and with full knowledge thereof, omitted to provide for any heirs or other individuals I may leave surviving. In the event that any such person should contest this Will, then in such event, I give, devise and bequeath to said person the sum of $1.00 (one dollar) and no more.

Nelson's Will is *not* a model of "artful draftsmanship" by the attorney who prepared it. For example, in the *in terrorem* clause above, it is hard to believe that Nelson would not have realized that his four children, to whom he gave his entire residuary estate, were exactly his "heirs." Perhaps the Will was intended to read "any *other* heirs."

After reading this Will, it is not surprising to learn from the papers filed with the Los Angeles County Superior Court that the original Will, which had apparently been left with the drafting attorney, was never located. A copy of Nelson's Will was finally admitted to probate. The adventures of Ricky Nelson had finally ended.

/S/ *Eric H. Nelson*

WILL DATED: August 22, 1985
Signed at Encino, California

Vladimir Horowitz

Date and Place of Birth	Date and Place of Death
October 1, 1903 Kiev, Russia	November 5, 1989 14 East 94th Street New York, New York

High Strung

His death certificate states simply that his "usual occupation" was as "pianist," and that his "business" was "music," but Vladimir Horowitz had few peers as a virtuoso at the piano. Horowitz was also known for his high-strung disposition and for his idiosyncratic interpretations of great musical compositions.

Horowitz was born to the cultured and wealthy Gorowitz family in Kiev, Russia. In 1925, young Vladimir left the Soviet Union on a student visa and then proceeded to take Europe by musical storm. For his Berlin debut in 1926, he changed his name from Gorowitz to Horowitz. Horowitz made his American debut in 1928. It was in 1933 that Horowitz met Wanda Toscanini, the daughter of famous conductor Arturo Toscanini. Wanda and Vladimir were married that same year. For the rest of the maestro's life, Wanda took charge of Horowitz's personal and professional affairs. In 1940, the couple settled permanently in New York. The magical Wanda was the one who made sure that Vladimir's favorite piano was moved to recitals, that special foods were prepared, and even that the hotel rooms Horowitz used be redecorated so that he would not be rattled by the change in his personal surroundings. The couple had a daughter, Sonya, in 1934, but she died in 1975.

Horowitz's Will manifests his devotion to his wife and his dedication to music. At the time of his death, Horowitz had amassed an estate worth between $6 million and $8 million, according to papers filed with the Surrogate's Court of New York. The bulk of that went to his surviving spouse, Wanda Toscanini Horowitz, outright, but there are also the following preresiduary bequests of interest:

> I hereby give, bequeath and devise to Yale University School of Music, New Haven, Connecticut, for inclusion in and subject to the terms of, the Horowitz Archive established pursuant to an Agreement dated August 14, 1987, all of my memorabilia, musical scores, correspondence, recital transcriptions, photographs, awards and trophies, programs and similar items relating to my musical career, all of which are presently contained in the library and other rooms of my residence at 14 East 94th Street.

Over the course of Vladimir's prolonged and prolific career, no doubt there was a lot of "memorabilia."

There was also a $200,000 outright bequest to Horowitz's "friend and companion, GIULIANA B. LOPES of Queens, New York." Ms. Lopes was described as a longtime employee of the Horowitzes'. If wife Wanda had not survived, then Ms. Lopes was to get an additional $300,000 outright.

In his Will, Horowitz also made the following unusual conditional bequest to the famous New York music school, Juilliard:

> To the Juilliard School of Music, New York, New York, the sum of Three Hundred Thousand ($300,000) dollars, such sum to be used for one or more scholarships for promising piano students who shall have the need for such financial assistance in order to continue their

artistic training, <u>provided that</u> such institution ac-<u>knowledges that, by accepting</u> such bequest, <u>it agrees</u> <u>never to hold any piano or other musical competition</u> <u>in my name or honor.</u> [emphasis added]

An unusual bequest by one of musical history's most eccentric virtuosos.

If wife Wanda had not survived, then Juilliard was to receive an additional $200,000 "subject to the conditions and proviso set forth." The balance of the estate was to be left to the Columbia Presbyterian Medical Center Fund, Inc., "for use in carrying out research to prevent, treat or cure Cancer, Acquired Immune Deficiency Syndrome, Alzheimer's Disease or Mental Illness." Horowitz's sensitive charitable bequest never vested because Wanda survived. As might be expected, Horowitz appointed Wanda and his manager to act as the executors of his Will.

Though the Will is silent on the issue of burial, Horowitz reportedly left instructions that he wanted to be buried in the Toscanini family plot in the Cimitero Monumentale in Milan, Italy.

/S/ **Vladimir Horowitz**

WILL DATED: November 1, 1988
Signed at 14 East 94th Street, New York, New York

THE COMEDIANS

Last Laughs

The Comedian	Date of Death
W. C. Fields Last Call for Alcohol	December 25, 1946
Jack Benny Not Thirty-nine Anymore	December 26, 1974
Groucho Marx "You Bet Your Life"	August 19, 1977
John Belushi Singing the Blues	March 5, 1982
Phil Silvers Do-it-yourself Special	November 1, 1985
Jackie Gleason "And Away We Go . . ."	June 24, 1987

W. C. Fields

Date and Place of Birth

January 29, 1880
Philadelphia, Pennsylvania

Date and Place of Death

December 25, 1946
Pasadena, California

Last Call for Alcohol

Commonly reported to have requested that his tombstone bear the inscription "I would rather be here than in Philadelphia" (the city of his birth), W. C. Fields, one of the great comic actors of all time, left a Will that includes no such instruction. The Will does, however, include the following fascinating provisions regarding Fields's directions for his own funeral:

> I direct my executors immediately upon the certificate of my death being signed to have my body placed in an inexpensive coffin and taken to a cemetery and cremated, and since I do not wish to cause my friends undue inconvenience or expense I direct my executors not to have any funeral or other ceremony or to permit anyone to view my remains, except as is necessary to furnish satisfactory proof of my death.

Fields, who died with an estate reportedly worth close to $800,000 in 1946, expressly requested that he be buried in an "inexpensive coffin" and that he be cremated as soon as possible.

Fields was named William Claude Dukenfield at his birth in Philadelphia. Apparently Fields put down his "Dukes" along the way because his Will begins, "I, WILLIAM C.

93

FIELDS, also known as W. C. FIELDS, also known as BILL FIELDS, residing at 2015 DeMille Drive, Los Angeles..." In the end, Fields signs his Will with his trademark initials "W. C." and last name.

Perhaps most fascinating about the disposition of Fields's estate are the provisions in the letter that he signed on the same day he signed his Will, which follows this piece. This detailed description of Fields's personal property illustrates many things about him, especially his love for things alcoholic. Fields died of cirrhosis of the liver, among other maladies, while he was in a sanitarium in Pasadena, California.

With a meticulous inventory such as that, it seems that Fields did not want to omit any articles of his property, including his treasured bottles of Shalimar perfume, which were apparently kept in the closet.

In his Will, Fields clearly favors two of his four siblings. He gave bequests of $5,000 to both his sister Adel C. Smith and his brother Walter Dukenfield, "also known as Walter Fields," and they are also both beneficiaries of a residuary trust, receiving weekly allowances of $60 and $75 respectively. As for his sister Elsie May and brother LeRoy Russell Dukenfield, Fields appears to have lost touch with them because the Will recites their "last known" addresses and he gave them each only token $500 bequests.

Upon the deaths of Adel, Walter, and Fields's friend and "nursemaid" Carlotta Monti, the property remaining in the trust was to be distributed as follows:

> I direct that my executors procure the organization of a membership or other approved corporation under the name W. C. FIELDS COLLEGE for orphan white boys and girls, where no religion of any sort is to be preached. Harmony is the purpose of this thought...

If "harmony" were truly the purpose of this thought, one wonders why it was restricted to white orphans. Ultimately, no orphans got any money because Fields's estranged wife, Harriet (aka Hattie), whom Fields had married in 1900 and never divorced, contested the Will and won. It is interesting that Fields does make the following bequest in his Will for his wife and son, but does not refer to them as such:

> To Hattie Fields and W. Claude Fields, now residing at 123½ North Gale Drive, Beverly Hills, California, the sum of Twenty Thousand Dollars to be divided equally.

In an attempt to deter any contest of the Will, Fields included the following provision: "I wish to disinherit anyone who in any way tries to confuse or break this Will or who contributes in any way to break this Will." In light of the ultimate victory of his wife and son over his estate, Fields looks like the sucker, and his wife and son got the break.

/S/ W. C. Fields

WILL DATED: April 28, 1943
Will signed at Los Angeles, California

2015 DeMille Drive,
Hollywood, California

To my Executor, Magda Michael:

In subparagraph 16 of the Third Paragraph of my last will
and testament, executed today, I bequeath to you in trust
the following articles of furniture and personal effects,
for delivery to the following persons:

To Charles Beyer: My desk, chair, chest, waste basket,
                    desk, knick-knacks, side table for
                    telephone, one open book case, revolving
                    book case, two wood baskets by fireplace,
                    Executone set, large steel cabinet and
                    contents, camera (he gave me) one-third
                    liquor, golf bag and clubs, one-third
                    ties, square trunk in basement contain-
                    ing books of press notices and programs,
                    also all the books of press notices and
                    programs upstairs, garden furniture,
                    station wagon, decanter set, 3 birdcage
                    stands, 2 ladders, ice chest, champagne
                    bucket.

To Carlotta Monti: One typewriter, red Taylor Trunk, large
                    Webster's Unabridged Dictionary, my small
                    dictionary and Roget's Thesaurus, Packard
                    Bell radio, with recording equipment,
                    one open book case, Encyclopedia Brit-
                    tanica, electric clock, secret filing
                    cabinet ("Secretaire") rubber mattress,
                    picture of me in Honolulu, one set of
                    gold dishes in closet, one set of gold
                    lamps in closet, blue Angora knit robe,
                    smaller steel cabinet in office, secre-
                    tary's desk and chair, two bottles Shalimar
                    in closet, large pair field glasses (Zephyr
                    7x35) share silverware in trunk and kitchen-
                    ware with Adele Clines, Frigidaire, water
                    softener, fireless cooker, 1 croquet set,
                    1 umbrella, records, 1 foot heater, electric
                    steam table, large safe, rubbing table, also
                    my 16-cylinder Cadillac limousine.

To Brother Walter Fields: General Electric portable radio,
traveling clock, one-half remaining trunks in basement,
one-third neckties (first choice) all of my clothes, shoes,
underwear, shirts, one third of my liquor, one rubbing
table, 2 car trunks, 2 auto robes, billiard table & chairs,
ping pong table.

To Sister Adel Smith: Waterbury ships clock, one-half of the
remaining trunks in basement, 2 bottles of Shalimar.

To Magda Michael: One typewriter, large dictaphone, 1 croquet set,
1 umbrella, 1 food heater.

To Gregory LaCava: revolvers, one third liquor, large electric
fan, pictures taken in Soboba, one set of
gold dishes in closet, one set gold lamps
in closet, electric refrigerator on wheels.

To Adele Vallery Clines: All the glasses upstairs and down,
washing machine (Bendix) silverware
in trunk and kitchen ware (share with
Carlotta Monti) bottle of Shalimar,
square glass ash tray, ash stands,
2 fly catchers, adjustable square
tables in office.

To Bob Murphy: Pictures in rubbing room, 1/2 Decker pictures

To Hershal Crockett: Double pen set on my desk and brown pencil
to match.

To Frank Clines: Paint spray gun and equipment, all paints,
big jack, carpenter tools, etc.

To Gene Fowler: Howard heating cabinet, all my pens and
pencils except those before mentioned,
also my small dictaphone, small leather trunk
and contents.

To Dave Chasen: 1/2 Decker pictures.

To Bob Howard: 2 wooden chairs in office, rocking chair, bar
chairs and fixtures.

To all my friends, herein mentioned: Distribute the wooden
paper holders I had made.

To George Moran: My jewelry, cuff links, tie clips and chains.

If lease of house cannot be broken, my brother Walter, or sister
Adel Smith or Carlotta Monti or Magda Michael may occupy it until
end of first year.

Dated this 28 day
of April, 1943.   W. C. Fields

Jack Benny

Date and Place of Birth	**Date and Place of Death**
February 14, 1894 Chicago, Illinois	December 26, 1974 Beverly Hills, California

Not Thirty-nine Anymore

*O*riginally named Benjamin Kubelsky, Jack Benny was given his first violin at age eight. For the rest of Benny's seventy-year-plus career, the violin became his signature prop, which he used more as an instrument to evoke laughter than to create music. Jack Benny's success with the violin led him to collect at least two valuable violins, a Stradivarius and a Presenda, about which Benny's Will states:

> I declare that I have heretofore made a gift of my Presenda and Stradivarius violins during my lifetime to the Los Angeles Philharmonic Orchestra, reserving only a life interest therein, and I direct my executors to deliver said violins to the aforesaid donee thereof.

By arranging to have Benny reserve only a life interest in the violins, Benny's attorneys may have been able to avoid having that valuable property taxed to his estate. In a similar tax-saving vein, the Will continues,

> My wife and I have similarly made an inter vivos gift of two paintings owned by us, namely, "La Charette de

Paille, Montfouchault" by Camille Pissarro and "Mont-
martre et Sacre Coeur" by Maurice Utrillo to the Los
Angeles County Museum of Art, reserving a life interest
therein for our joint lifetimes. If I survive my wife, I
direct my Executor to deliver said paintings to said Museum.

Of course, one could not conceive of Jack Benny ever uttering
such words, but his lawyers were paid to put them in his
mouth.

Perennially claiming to be only thirty-nine years old, Jack
Benny's humor depended upon people's common concerns
and faults, including lying about their age and penny-
pinching. Apparently his penny-pinching paid off, as Jack died
with an estate reported to be worth over $4 million, according
to papers filed with the court. Benny's Will contains a bequest
of $20,000 to his sister, Florence Fenchal, and a relatively
modest bequest of $10,000 to the Motion Picture and Tele-
vision Fund. The bulk of his estate was to be held in trust for
the benefit of his surviving widow, Mary Benny, and to a
lesser degree for the benefit of his sister, daughter, and grandchildren. Mary Benny was named as co-executor of the Will
to act with Benny's attorney.

Perhaps wanting to "die up to" his reputation for penny-
pinching, Benny includes a one-dollar *in terrorem* clause in
his Will, which concludes as follows:

If any heir-at-law, next of kin, or devisee, legatee or
beneficiary under this Will shall contest it or any of its
parts or provisions, any share or interest given to that
person shall be revoked and become void, and in that
event, I bequeath to any such person the sum of ONE
DOLLAR ($1.00) only.

Maybe the penny-pinching Jack Benny believed that even "ONE DOLLAR" was too much.

/S/ *Jack Benny*

WILL DATED: June 26, 1974
WILL SIGNED: Beverly Hills, California

Groucho Marx

Date and Place of Birth	Date and Place of Death
October 2, 1890 East 93rd Street New York, New York	August 19, 1977 Cedars Sinai Medical Center Los Angeles, California

"You Bet Your Life"

As his Will makes evident, comedian Groucho (a/k/a Julius) Marx was the self-appointed victim of three ex-wives. The second article of Groucho's Will states:

> I declare that I am not married; that I have had three former wives, to-wit, RUTH GARRITY (formerly RUTH MARX), CATHERINE MARIE MARX (also known as KAY MARIE MARX), and EDNA MARIE MARX (formerly known as EDNA MARIE HIGGINS and also as EDEN HARTFORD), from whom I have been divorced by final decree. I have three children, namely, my son, ARTHUR J. MARX, my daughter, MIRIAM RUTH MARX, and my daughter, MELINDA MARX.... Except as above specified, I have never been married and have no children.

Later in the Will, Marx reiterates, "I have, except as otherwise stated in this will, intentionally and with full knowledge omitted to provide for my heirs living at the time of my decease. Moreover, except for the trust established in Article SIXTH, I expressly disinherit my ex-wives." The trust referred to was $25,000 placed in trust for the benefit of his ex-wife Catherine Marie Marx and provides for the payment to her of the grand sum of $100 per week.

Groucho married his first wife, Ruth Johnson, in 1920, and his son, Arthur, and daughter Miriam were the issue of that marriage, which ended in divorce in 1942. In 1945, Groucho married Catherine Gorcey. That marriage produced his daughter Melinda before ending in divorce in 1950. Groucho's third marriage was to twenty-four-year-old model Eden Hartford in 1953 when Groucho was on the other side of sixty. That marriage ended in 1969 as Eden was hitting forty, and Groucho was looking at eighty.

After three strikes, Groucho never remarried. However, in 1972 he began publicly appearing with his attractive "secretary-companion," Erin Fleming. In Groucho's twilight years, his mental competence came into question, and he became the object of a messy conservatorship proceeding involving Miss Fleming and Groucho's family. Ultimately, Groucho's grandson, Andrew, was named Groucho's permanent conservator until Groucho's death.

Groucho's Will makes the following interesting provisions for the disposition of some his personal property:

A. I give and bequeath to the Smithsonian Institution, Washington, D.C. all of my memorabilia, including items such as scrapbooks, still pictures, scripts and film materials (but not the intangible property rights therein), my Academy Award statuette, my French medal, and such other items as ERIN FLEMING determines to constitute the collection of memorabilia; provided, however, that prior to the gift to the Smithsonian Institution, subject to approval of ERIN FLEMING, each of my children may select from among the memorabilia such items as each desires, and I hereby give to each of them the items so selected, as tokens of my affection.
B. I give to ERIN FLEMING...the Boutonnière of the Commander des Arts et Lettres presented to me by the French government.

C. I give to GODDARD LIEBERSON, if he survives me, that painting in my home depicting myself and my brothers, painted by John Decker.

D. I direct my executors to sell as soon as reasonably convenient all remaining items of jewelry, books, pictures, paintings, works of art, furniture, furnishings, fixtures and personal effects, together with my home at 1083 Hillcrest Road, Beverly Hills, California...

Despite the foregoing bequests and a cash bequest to Miss Fleming of $150,000, she filed a claim against the estate for approximately $75,000, according to papers filed with the court. The Bank of America National Trust and Savings Association, which was named as the sole executor of the Groucho Marx estate, rejected Miss Fleming's claim. There was additional legal skirmishing over the estate between Marx's children and Miss Fleming, which was widely reported by the press.

Marx was generous with others named in his Will. He gave $50,000 to each of his brothers who survived him (only Zeppo), and $5,000 to each of his grandchildren living at the time of his death. He rewarded a cousin of one of his ex-wives with a bequest in the amount of $3,500 "because she has been so kind to my daughter Melinda."

Despite his apparent generosity, Marx's Will also utilizes the feared *in terrorem* clause. Pursuant to the provisions of the Will, if a bequest were forfeited by any beneficiary, it was to be paid instead to the Jewish Federation Council of Greater Los Angeles.

Finally, for the man who once remarked that he would not want to be a member of any club that would accept him as a member, Groucho specifically bequeaths his membership in the Hillcrest Country Club to his son, Arthur. According to papers filed by the estate with the Los Angeles County court, that Hillcrest Country Club membership had an appraised value of $20,000 in Marx's estate, which had a reported value of almost $2 million. Apparently, Groucho said the magic words many times.

/S/ *Julius H. Marx*
/S/ *Groucho Marx*

WILL DATED: *September 24, 1974*
Signed in Beverly Hills, California

John Belushi

Date and Place of Birth

January 24, 1949
Wheaton, Illinois

Date and Place of Death

March 5, 1982
Chateau Marmont
Hollywood, California

Singing the Blues

Manic comic John Belushi had married his high school girlfriend, Judith Jacklin, on New Year's Eve in 1976. The couple had no children at the time of Belushi's death six years later. Pursuant to the second article of his Will, Belushi's entire estate was left to Judith, if she survived him, which she did.

If Judith had not survived her husband, the estate was to be divided into eleven equal parts with shares given outright, or in trust, to the following relatives of Belushi and his wife: Belushi's father, Adam; mother, Agnes; sister, Marion; brother, James; brother, William; nephew, Adam; father-in-law, Robert L. Jacklin; mother-in-law, Jean Jacklin; brother-in-law, Robert B. Jacklin; sister-in-law, Pamela Jacklin; and sister-in-law, Patricia Brewster.

Because Judith Jacklin Belushi survived her husband, none of these surviving relatives inherited anything from Belushi's estate. Belushi's Will also contained a comprehensive *in terrorem* clause, but with the entire estate passing to his wife, there would be no one who could realistically contest his Will. Dying at a young age, Belushi's twenty-two-page, detailed Will seems eerily unnecessary.

After his death from a drug overdose in Hollywood's infamous Chateau Marmont Hotel, Belushi was buried in Abel's

Hill Cemetery on Martha's Vineyard near the home Belushi and his wife owned. Leading the funeral procession in black leather on a motorcycle was Belushi's close friend Dan Aykroyd, who was singing the blues without Blues Brother Belushi.

/S/ John A. Belushi

WILL DATED: March 23, 1979
Residing at 60 Morton Street, New York, New York

Phil Silvers

Date and Place of Birth	Date and Place of Death
1912 Brooklyn, New York	November 1, 1985 Los Angeles, California

Do-it-yourself Special

Comedian Phil Silvers was best known for his role as the conniving and scheming Sergeant Ernie Bilko on "The Phil Silvers Show," a popular 1950s television series. With his overbearing yet winning personality, Silvers could make his villainous characters lovable. In his last years, Silvers appeared regularly on the variety and talk-show circuit.

What follows is an exact transcription of Phil Silver's Will and codicil in toto, which were handwritten and obviously prepared without the assistance of an attorney. Despite inconsistencies and misspellings in the Will and codicil, they were admitted to probate by the Los Angeles County Superior Court. Letters testamentary were issued to Phil's eldest daughter, Tracey, and attorney David Flynn. The Will speaks for itself, but one noteworthy bequest is for $5,000 to his "nurse and constant companion" for her consideration during his long illness. Phil had had a stroke 1973, and he himself described his medical condition as "shaky."

Silvers's Will concludes: "I go to my God knowing at least as a comedian I was one of a kind." So was his Will.

/S/ Phil

WILL DATED: July 4, 1984

1

Phil Silvers

(July 4th 1984)

This handwritten document
will serve as my last will and testament
I request for David Flynn of the firm of Traubner & Flynn to
share the duties of Executor with my eldest daughter Tracey

For carrying out my requests they are to receive and share
the sum of Five thousand dollars $2500 each

Excluding the following bequests I leave my entire fortune
to be shares equally by my five daughters namely Tracey,
Nancey, Cathy, Candace and Laury. This legacy includes my
ownership of all Stock and Bodns, Bank accounts, securities
and monies in banks and possible partial ownerships such as
the television series "Gilligan Island" - My many awards and
documents, photos, and memophilia should be shared equally
by my five above mentioned daughters, this is to be supervised by my eldest child Tracey

My further requests
To my sister Mrs Pearl Sabin of 200 W 54th St New York City
10014
the sum of Fifteen Thousand dollars $15,000
To my brother Bob Silver 1120 Brighter Beach Ave
Brooklyn, N.Y.
11235

Fifteen thousand dollars $1500
In the event both the above my Brother and Sister are not
alive to accept this legacy both Sums $30,000 Thirty thou-
sand in Total should be awarded my Nephew Saul Silver
390 First Ave
New York City
N.Y. 10010

Pg 2

Phil Silvers

To my friend Leo de Lyon 13147 Hartland Dr. No
Hollywood, CA 91605 To Leo I bequest the Sum of Five
Thousand dollars $5000 and with this sum my deep respect
and love - To my nurse and constant companion

> Mrs. Jean Edward
> 109348 Eucaplyus
> Apt. E
> Hawthorne
> CA 90250
> Phone no. 978-8989

   I bequeth to Mrs Edwards the sum of Five
Thousand Dollars $5000 small payment for her
many considerations during my long illness

   I have made no reference to my ex wife Evelyn Patrick
early in our marriage there were some years and there are
five children will attest however for reasons best to the both
of us I leave her nothing material in my also no bitterness
At this writing she is doing very well in her well prepared
profession and I wish her well

   Any reference to the validity of my mental alertness
can be attested by my Doctor of many years

   Clarence M. Agress 553-2021 he kept me going when
my physical condition was shaky following a stroke in 1973

   I request my daughter Tracey to inform the
media of my passing and to arrange my funeral
in Forest Lawn I want a simple coffin and a small
headstone inscribed Phil Silvers Comedian

3

Phil Silvers

I expect David Flynn and TRACY to inform the media and if
possible I would appreciate a small Eulogue
delivered by my friend of many years
Milton Berle. I request my funeral arrangments
coffin and head stone not to exceed the sum of
Ten thousand dollars $10,000
   Good by I go to my rest willingly
The last years were painful but were made
bearable by friends I made through the years
especially Ed Traubner who smmothed out
many a curve
   I go to my God knowing at least as
a comedian I was only one of a kind
          Shalom
           Phil

Jackie Gleason

Date and Place of Birth	**Date and Place of Death**
February 26, 1916	June 24, 1987
Brooklyn, New York	Fort Lauderdale, Florida

"And Away We Go . . ."

Born in Brooklyn, New York, he was named Herbert John Gleason. His father, an insurance clerk, abandoned the family when "Jackie" was eight years old. Gleason's mother supported her son by working as a subway-booth attendant until she died in 1932 when Jackie was sixteen. Gleason's show business career rose steadily from his winning amateur talent contests, to working as a "barker" in carnivals, to small parts in films, to acting on Broadway, and ultimately entering the medium of television in its infancy in 1949. Gleason was one of television's most popular entertainers and had a prolonged honeymoon with the American public.

Jackie Gleason was best known as the scheming and bumbling bus driver, Ralph Kramden, in "The Honeymooners." Gleason had a reputation for being a big eater and big drinker, and it showed; his weight was reported to be in excess of 280 pounds at one time. His gregarious manners and larger-than-life ego gave him an inimitable comic style.

At the time of his death from cancer at the age of seventy-one, Gleason was survived by his third wife, Marilyn, and two daughters, Geraldine and Linda, from his first marriage. His thirty-five-year first marriage had ended in divorce in 1971 when he married Beverly McKittrick, a former secretary. That marriage lasted until 1974, when he was divorced from Ms.

McKittrick and subsequently married Marilyn Taylor Horwich.

Most interesting about Jackie Gleason's Will is not the Will itself but the codicil, which was executed the day before he died. In that codicil, dated June 23, 1987, Gleason increased the bequest to "my longtime secretary SYDELL SPEAR" from $25,000 to $100,000. However, due to his debilitating illness, Gleason was not able to sign his own name on the codicil; he directed another to sign his name for him in the presence of two witnesses.

The balance of Gleason's estate was divided among Gleason's wife and two daughters.

For the comedian who often referred to himself as "the Great One," it is not surprising that in the first section of his Will he authorizes his "personal representatives" (the name for executors under Florida law) to spend as much as they want on "funeral expenses, the acquisition of a burial site, the erection of a suitable headstone or monument over my grave ... without regard to any provision of law limiting such expenditures." It seems that the Great One did not want to go unnoticed, even in the cemetery.

/S/ Herbert John Gleason

WILL DATED: April 11, 1985
WILL SIGNED AT: 3425 Willow Wood Road, Lauderhill, Florida
CODICIL DATED: June 23, 1987

THE SHOWMEN

The Show Must Go On

The Showman	Date of Death
Harry Houdini No Escape	October 31, 1926
George M. Cohan Born on the 4th of July, Dead on the 5th	November 5, 1942
Liberace Flame Buoyant	February 4, 1987
Fred Astaire Last Dance	June 22, 1987
Bob Fosse Dinner's on Me	September 23, 1987

Harry Houdini

Date and Place of Birth	Date and Place of Death
April 6, 1874 Brooklyn, New York	October 31, 1926 (Halloween) Detroit, Michigan

No Escape

The world-famous magician and great escape artist known simply as Houdini was originally named Ehrich Weiss at birth and was the son of a rabbi. At the age of nine, Houdini joined a traveling circus as a contortionist and trapeze performer, and the rest is mystery.

At a young age, Houdini became a celebrated figure throughout America and earned large sums of money for performing in vaudeville acts and winning bets. His most famous escape was from his own self-styled torture chamber, in which he was shackled head down in a tank full of water. Contrary to popular belief, Houdini did not die in one of those chambers but in a hospital in Detroit, as the result of complications resulting from an appendix operation. The appendicitis was the result of a hard blow to Houdini's appendix delivered by a college student whom Houdini had just lectured on spiritualistic tricks and Houdini's own physical prowess.

During his lifetime Houdini collected an extensive library devoted to magic, spiritualism, and the black arts. When he died in 1926, that book collection was valued at $500,000, according to *The New York Times*. Under his Will, Houdini bequeaths his library relating to "spiritualism, occultism and psychical research to the Congressional Library at Washington" and his "collection of books, pamphlets, letters and the

like related to spiritualism, occultism and psychical research"
to the "American Society for Psychical Research."

However, in the hastily drawn codicil to his Will, Houdini
revokes the bequest to the Society as follows:

> I...wish to cancel the codicil giving my Spiritualistic
> library to the American Society of Psychic Research,
> the entire collection is to go with my Magical Library
> to the Congressional Library in Washington. The reason
> I object giving my Spiritualistic library to the American
> Society of Psychical Research is because I object to a
> dishonorable person like J. Malcolm Bird being con-
> nected with any reputable organization.

Obviously, Houdini believed J. Malcolm to be a strange
bird.

Perhaps most interesting about Harry Houdini's Will is the
consideration that he gives to his own burial. During his life
he had always said that if there were any way to come back
from the dead he would, so his burial arrangements required
special consideration. Under the nineteenth article of his Will,
Houdini directs that upon his death his body

> be embalmed and buried in the same manner in which
> my beloved mother was buried upon her death, and that
> my grave be constructed in a vault in the same manner
> as my beloved mother's last resting place was con-
> structed for her burial; and I also direct that I shall be
> buried in the grave immediately alongside of that of my
> dear departed mother....

What a field day Sigmund Freud would have had with that
one.

Houdini also provided that "the bronze bust of me, made
by Cassidy of Manchester, England, shall be put on the exedra
erected by me in said cemetery in the place provided for it

on such exedra." An "exedra" is a porch or portico adjacent
to the grave; apparently, Houdini wanted to be sure that his
returning spirit found the right tomb.

Despite Houdini's magical powers, there appears to have
been significant domestic strife within the Weiss family. In
one section of his Will, Houdini expressly disinherits a woman
named Sadie Glantz Weiss, "the divorced wife of my brother
Nathan Joseph Weiss and the present wife of my brother, Dr.
Leopold David Weiss."

Houdini bequeathed all of his "household effects, furniture,
trophies, silverware, ornaments, jewelry, diamonds and personal effects, including my oil paintings" and one-sixth of his
residuary estate to his wife, Wilhelmina Rahner Houdini. He
also appointed his wife to be the executor of his Will. Bankers
Trust Company was named as a successor executor.

As was appropriate for the doyen of magicians, in his Will
Houdini made a bequest of $1,000 to the Society of American
Magicians.

/S/ *Harry Houdini*
formerly Ehrich Weiss

WILL DATED: July 30, 1924
RESIDING AT: 278 West 113th Street, New York, New York
CODICIL DATED: May 6, 1925

George M. Cohan

Date and Place of Birth	Date and Place of Death
July 4, 1878 Providence, Rhode Island	November 5, 1942 993 Fifth Avenue New York, New York

Born on the 4th of July,
Dead on the 5th

America's favorite Yankee-Doodle Dandy of the stage, George M. Cohan once stated, "I can write better plays than any living dancer and dance better than any living playwright."

Cohan seemed to have had American patriotism in his stars, as he was, in fact, born on the 4th of July to Helen and Jeremiah Cohan, who worked the vaudeville circuit. For a while, the family performed as "the Four Cohans," including George's sister Josephine. During the "gay nineties," Cohan was best remembered for his nightly farewell on stage: "My mother thanks you, my father thanks you, my sister thanks you, and I thank you."

Cohan's first wife was named Ethel Levey and was his dancing partner after sister Josephine danced off to get married. George and Ethel had one daughter, named Georgette. In 1907 that marriage ended. On his birthday in 1908, Cohan married Agnes Mary Nolan Cohan, who was by his bedside when he died thirty-four years later. Together, George and Agnes had three children: Helen Frances, Mary Helen, and George Michael Cohan, Jr.

In his Will, Cohan provides equally for his four children

and his wife, Agnes. Each got 5 percent of his substantial estate outright, and each was the beneficiary of a trust holding the remaining 75 percent of the estate. Cohan takes pains to defend the equal gift to Mrs. Cohan with the following paragraph in his Will:

> Because of my beloved wife having registered in our joint names, with the right of survivorship, a substantial amount of my securities which will become her property in the event of my dying before her, I respectfully request that she accept the provisions that I herein make for her in lieu of her right to elect her statutory rights against the provisions of this will.

According to papers filed with the surrogate's court, Mrs. Cohan complied with her husband's "respectful" request.

Cohan appointed "my friend and legal counselor of many years, DENNIS F. O'BRIEN," as executor of his Will and co-trustee of the residuary trust. Cohan, who was known to be quite shrewd about protecting the value of his copyrights, also provided the following in his Will:

> (a) It is my intention to convey to a corporation that I plan to organize in the near future title to all of the literary compositions, dramatic compositions, dramatico-musical compositions, musical compositions and songs and all copyrights that I may own in connection with such compositions...
> (b) I respectfully request those persons who are authorized to renew copyrights of any of my literary compositions, dramatic compositions, dramatico-musical compositions, musical compositions and songs pursuant to the rights of renewal of such copyrights, to procure such renewals of copyrights...
> (c) I respectfully request that such moneys as may be payable to me from the American Society of Composers,

Authors and Publishers be paid to the executor of my estate...

One doesn't hear too much about "dramatico-musical compositions" these days, but Cohan did not want to miss a beat, or a royalty.

Toward its conclusion, the Will states Cohan's "wish" that title to the copyrights of all his compositions be retained and never sold. Cohan points out that the request is "based upon my experience of many years in dealing with the licenses to use and turn to account the literary compositions, dramatic compositions, dramatico-musical compositions, musical compositions and songs that I have originated, written and composed."

After a prolific songwriting career spanning over fifty years, Cohan certainly had quite a lot of copyright to protect. Now that's the spirit of a dandy Yankee!

/S/ George M. Cohan

WILL DATED: March 2, 1939
CODICIL DATED: October 23, 1941

Liberace

Date and Place of Birth	Date and Place of Death
May 16, 1919	February 4, 1987
635 51st Street	Riverside County
West Allis, Wisconsin	Palm Springs, California

Flame Buoyant

I, LIBERACE, also sometimes known as WALTER VAL-
ENTINO LIBERACE, LEE LIBERACE and WLADSIU VAL-
ENTINO LIBERACE, domiciled, in Las Vegas Nevada,
being of sound and disposing mind and memory, do
hereby make, publish and declare this to be my LAST
WILL AND TESTAMENT.

Flamboyant, glitzy, happy-go-lucky, and gay pianist Liberace had a decidedly dry Will. The Will begins with the
following sentence under the seemingly inappropriate head-
ing "Marital and Family Status": "I declare that I am unmarried and have no living issue." Anybody who had ever seen
Liberace "perform" could probably have told you that. Liberace was never married in a formal sense, although his liaisons with a host of male companions have been widely
reported. In 1982, Scott Thorson, who had been Liberace's
companion, chauffeur, and "bodyguard," sued the guarded
body for over $100 million. According to published reports,
that suit was settled for $95,000, or less than one-tenth of one
percent of the total amount originally sought.

According to his Will, which was signed thirteen days before
he died, Liberace transferred his entire estate "to JOEL R.

STROTE, as Trustee, or any successor Trustee of the trust designated as 'THE LIBERACE REVOCABLE TRUST' established earlier this day, of which I am the Grantor and he is the original Trustee." Mr. Strote, who was Liberace's attorney, has stated that most of the Liberace estate will pass to the Liberace Foundation for the Performing and Creative Arts. Undoubtedly, Liberace's estate was quite substantial, as he had earned over $5 million per year for over twenty-five years, according to newspaper reports. That equals at least $125 million in lifetime earnings.

When he died, Liberace was survived by his sister, Ann Liberace Farrell, of Las Vegas, Nevada, niece Ina Mae Liberace, and nephews Lester Lee Liberace, Rudolph V. Liberace, and Harry Henry Liberace. Whether these Liberace relatives were beneficiaries of the trust established by Liberace about two weeks before he died only Joel R. Strote and a few others know for sure.

The cause of Liberace's death was officially termed "cardiac arrest due to congestive heart failure brought on by subacute encephalopathy . . . a contributing cause was aplastic anemia." After the flamboyant entertainer's death the Riverside County, California, coroner said that that was just an oblique way of saying that the death stemmed from AIDS, but that has repeatedly been denied by many of those closest to Liberace. Having lived a lifetime of fantasy and illusion, Liberace himself may not have wanted the specter of a dreaded disease to tarnish his gilded image.

/S/ *Liberace*

WILL DATED: January 22, 1987

Fred Astaire

Date and Place of Birth	Date and Place of Death
May 10, 1899 Omaha, Nebraska	June 22, 1987 Century City Hospital Los Angeles, California

Last Dance

Born Frederick Austerlitz in Omaha, Nebraska, Fred Astaire, "the Ultimate Dancer," appeared in vaudeville, on stage, screen, and television, and starred in over thirty musical films between 1933 and 1968. Offscreen, Astaire shunned the debonair top-hat-and-tails look that became his trademark. He was known as an affable and ordinary man, blessed with an extraordinary talent.

Astaire's first wife was Phyllis Livingston Potter, whom he married in 1933. The couple had two children together and she had one from a previous marriage. Phyllis died in 1954. Astaire's second wife, Robyn Smith, was more than forty-five years younger than Astaire when he married her in 1980 at the age of eighty one. Mrs. Smith was a jockey, and Astaire met her through his own interest in horses and his ownership of a stable. Seems like Fred wanted a new filly in his personal stable.

In his 1986 Will, Astaire describes his family relationships as follows:

My family includes my wife, ROBYN ASTAIRE, and my adult children by my first wife, PHYLLIS ASTAIRE, who died many years ago. The names of my children are FRED ASTAIRE, JR. and PHYLLIS AVA ASTAIRE

123

> McKENZIE. My stepson, ELIPHALET NOTT POTTER, is
> the son of my deceased wife PHYLLIS by a former mar-
> riage. Aside from the foregoing, all references in this
> Will are to ROBYN ASTAIRE.

Astaire named his son, Fred Astaire, Jr., stepson Eliphalet
Nott Potter, Jr., and an attorney as executors of his Will, and
as trustees of a trust that he had established with his first wife
in 1942. In addition to that 1942 trust, Astaire created another
inter vivos trust in 1985 that received his residuary estate
upon his death. In the event that two or all of the named
executors were not able to act, Astaire named his daughter,
Phyllis Ava Astaire McKenzie, to act as a successor executrix.
In deference to his wife, who was not named as an executrix,
the Will states:

> I request that my acting Executors consult with my wife
> ROBYN and obtain her approval prior to any disposi-
> tion proposed for my interest in Ava Productions, Inc.,
> or any of its assets, or my interests or royalties in spe-
> cial television properties which form part of my estate.

The last article of Astaire's Will succinctly states, "I direct
that my funeral be private and that there be no memorial
service." Without wanting any fanfare, dancer extraordinaire
Fred Astaire danced into the dark at the age of eighty-eight.

/S/ Fred Astaire

WILL DATED: January 16, 1986
Signed in Los Angeles, California

Bob Fosse

Date and Place of Birth	Date and place of Death
June 23, 1927 Chicago, Illinois	September 23, 1987 Washington University Hospital Washington, D.C.

Dinner's on Me

$\mathcal{I}$n 1973, Bob Fosse was the first person to win entertainment's triple crown, winning an Oscar as the director of the film *Cabaret*, a Tony Award for his direction of the play *Pippin* on Broadway, and an Emmy Award for his direction of the television special "Liza with a 'Z.'"

Known for his nonstop work habits and chain-smoking, Fosse's personal life was also a whirlwind affair. Fosse was married three times and was romantically linked with many women. Fosse's three wives were dancers and performers, Mary Ann Niles, Joan McCracken, and Gwen Verdon, and his girlfriends included actresses Jessica Lange and Ann Reinking.

Throughout his career Fosse worked with a variety of performers, and through his Will, Fosse remembers many of those with whom he worked, and played. Most unusual about the Will of Bob Fosse is the following bequest:

> I give and bequeath the sum of Twenty-Five Thousand ($25,000) Dollars to my Executor, to be distributed by him to the friends of mine listed, and in the amounts set forth, in a letter of instructions which I have delivered to him. I have made this provision so that when my friends receive this bequest they will go out and

<u>have dinner on me.</u> [emphasis added] They all have at one time or other during my life been very kind to me. I thank them.

Among the sixty-six people remembered by Fosse were the following well-known names from film and theater: actors Dustin Hoffman, Roy Scheider (who portrayed the Fosse character in *All That Jazz*), Ben Gazzara, and Ben Vereen; actresses Liza Minnelli, Ann Reinking, Melanie Griffith, Julie Hagerty, Janet Leigh, and Jessica Lange; writers E. L. Doctorow, Neil Simon, and Elia Kazan; and comedian Buddy Hackett. After the $25,000 bequest was equally divided among the sixty-six designated recipients, each one received the odd figure of $378.79 to "go out and have dinner on" Fosse. Even at the pricey restaurants that Fosse often frequented, that sum was enough to assure that no one on the list would go hungry.

In addition to the dinner allowances, Fosse made the following more substantial devises and bequests to certain people from his past and to two charitable causes of special interest to him:

A. To my friend and agent, SAMUEL COHN, if he shall survive me, all of my right, title and interest in and to the restaurant known as The Laundry and located in East Hampton, New York, in whatever form my interest in this business entity may take.

B. To my sister, MARIANNE DIMOS, if she shall survive me, the sum of Twenty Thousand ($20,000) Dollars.

C. To the HEART FUND, New York City Chapter, the sum of Fifteen Thousand ($15,000) Dollars.

D. To the POSTGRADUATE CENTER FOR MENTAL HEALTH, the sum of Fifteen Thousand ($15,000) Dollars.

E. To my assistant, CATHY NICOLAS [sic, "Nicholas"],

if she shall survive me, the sum of Fifteen Thousand
($15,000) Dollars.

F. To my friend, HERB GARDNER, if he shall survive
me, the sum of Fifteen Thousand ($15,000) Dollars.

G. To my former wife, MARY ANN NILES, if she shall
survive me, the sum of Fifteen Thousand ($15,000) Dol-
lars.

After Fosse survived a near-fatal heart attack in 1967, one
can well understand the motivation behind his gift to the
Heart Fund of New York. It is also heartwarming to see a gift
to Fosse's first wife, Mary Ann Niles, whom he had divorced
in 1951 but with whom he was still close. Coincidentally, Niles
died a few days after Fosse did.

In addition to those specific bequests, Fosse established a
$100,000 trust fund designated as the "Bob Fosse Theatre
Scholarship," which was to provide financial assistance for the
education and training in the theatrical arts for "deserving
individuals." In his Will Fosse states, "I have been motivated
to establish this fund because my life has been devoted to the
American theatre and its continued well-being and improve-
ment are of great importance to me." Fosse named Gwen
Verdon and his daughter, Nicole, as the trustees of this trust.

The final curtain for Bob Fosse came at approximately the
same time as the curtain was going up on the opening night
of the revival of his 1966 hit *Sweet Charity* at the National
Theatre in Washington. Prior to the opening, Fosse collapsed
from another heart attack in his room at the Willard Hotel in
Washington and was pronounced dead at the George Washington University Hospital shortly thereafter. At his side when
he died was his third wife and artistic collaborator, Gwen
Verdon. The cast of the show was not informed of Fosse's
death until the curtain went down at the end of the show after
a thunderous standing ovation from the audience. True to the
spirit of Bob Fosse, the show went on.

At the time of his death, Fosse's estate was reportedly worth close to $4 million and was divided equally between his wife, Gwen Verdon, and daughter, Nicole. The last act of Fosse's successful career was his Will, which included "sweet charity" and rewarded many of the people through whose lives Bob Fosse had danced.

/S/ Robert Fosse

WILL DATED: March 28, 1985
Residing at 58 West 58th Street, New York, New York

THE PRESIDENTS

All the Presidents' Ends

The President	Date of Death
George Washington Father of No One but Our Country	December 14, 1799
Thomas Jefferson Declaration of Dependents	July 4, 1826
Calvin Coolidge Short, and to the Point	January 5, 1933
Franklin D. Roosevelt Warm Springs Eternal	April 12, 1945
Harry Truman The Buck Stopped in Independence	December 26, 1972
John F. Kennedy "Mindful of the Uncertainty of Life"	November 22, 1963

George Washington

Date and Place of Birth	Date and Place of Death
February 22, 1732 Pope's Creek, Virginia	December 14, 1799 Mount Vernon, Virginia

Father of No One but Our Country

When he died in 1799, George Washington was reported to be one of the wealthiest men in the young nation. He owned more than 33,000 acres of land, including over 23,000 in Virginia, 5,000 in Kentucky, and large tracts in Maryland, New York, and the Northwest Territory. He owned corporate stocks worth over $25,000, and his livestock consisted of 640 sheep, 329 cows, horses, and mules.

Washington also owned hundreds of slaves. In the second item of his Will Washington reveals his personal thoughts on the slavery question. The Will states:

> Upon the decease of my wife, it is my Will & desire that all Slaves which I hold in my own right, shall receive their freedom....And whereas among those who will receive freedom according to this devise, there may be some, who from old age or bodily infirmities, and others who on account of their infancy, that will be unable to support themselves; it is my Will and desire that all ... shall be comfortably cloathed & fed by my heirs while they live....And I do expressly forbid the Sale, or transportation out of the said Commonwealth of Virginia, of any Slave I may die possessed of, under any pretence whosoever....And to my Mulatto man William (calling himself William Lee) I give immediate freedom; or if he

131

> should prefer it (on account of the accidents which have befallen him, and which have rendered him incapable of walking or of any active employment) to remain in the situation he now is.... This I give him as a testimony of my sense of his attachment to me, and for his faithful services during the Revolutionary War.

At the age of twenty-seven, George Washington had married Martha Dandridge Curtis, a wealthy Virginia widow who had two children from her prior marriage. Martha Washington outlived her husband, dying in 1802, and she is his primary beneficiary under his Will. Under item one of the Will he gives her a life interest in almost his entire estate as well as outright gifts, including the "liquors and groceries" that were on hand at the time of his decease.

George Washington died without having any natural children. Nonetheless he treated his nephews and nieces and wife's prior children with paternal affection. Under the third article of his Will Washington states:

> And whereas it has always been my intention, since my expectation of having issue has ceased, to consider the Grand children of my wife in the same light as I do my own relations...more especially by the two whom we have reared from their earliest infancy...I give & bequeath...the residue of my Mount Vernon Estate, not already devised to my Nephew Bushrod Washington.

In addition to Martha, George provided for many relatives and friends under his Will. He left his famous home, Mount Vernon, to his nephew Bushrod Washington. Other bequests include the following:

> **Item** To my Nephew Bushrod Washington, I give and bequeath all the Papers in my possession, which relate to my Civel and Military Administration of the affairs

of this Country;—I leave to him also, such of my private Papers as are worth preserving.

Item To my brother Charles Washington I give & bequeath the gold headed Cane left me by Doctr. Franklin in his Will....To General de la Fayette I give a pair of finely wrought steel Pistols, taken from the enemy in the Revolutionary War.

The bulk of Washington's land-rich estate was to be sold, with the proceeds to be divided among twenty-three friends and relatives. Washington named his ailing wife, Martha, and five male members of his family—William Augustine Washington, George Steptoe Washington, Samuel Washington, Lawrence Lewis, and the ubiquitous Bushrod—to be his executors. After naming his executors, Washington cautioned that "having endeavored to be plain, and explicit in all the Devises—even at the expense of prolixity, perhaps of tautology, I hope, and trust, that no disputes will arise concerning them." Despite this admonition Washington's Will provides a mechanism for any disputes to be arbitrated by three "impartial and intelligent men, known for their probity and good understanding."

Regarding the plans for his burial and funeral, Washington's Will states:

The family Vault at Mount Vernon requiring repairs, and being improperly situated besides, I desire that a new one of Brick, and upon a larger Scale may be built ...And it is my express desire that my Corpse may be Interred in a private manner, without—parade, or funeral Oration.

Perhaps one secret to Washington's great leadership ability was his modesty and lack of ostentation.

Washington signed his Will in the summer before his death in 1799. The date he wrote at the end of the Will incorrectly omits the word *nine* and that explains the inconsistency with his final remark that the Will was being signed in the twenty-fourth year from the date of United States independence in 1776. Perhaps Washington was tired at the end of his illustrious and incomparable career, and after having written the thirty-page Will by hand.

/S/ G. Washington

WILL DATED: July 9, 1790 [*sic*, "1799"]
Will signed at Mount Vernon, Virginia

Thomas Jefferson

Date and Place of Birth	Date and Place of Death
April 13, 1743 Shadwell, Virginia	July 4, 1826 Monticello, Virginia

Declaration of Dependents

When he died on the fiftieth anniversary of the signing of the Declaration of Independence, which he had drafted at the age of thirty-three, Thomas Jefferson was a debt-ridden man. Jefferson was known to have an extravagant lifestyle and to be quite generous with those who sought his assistance.

The following excerpts from the Will and codicil were signed only a few months before Jefferson's death at the age of eighty-three. Jefferson had been a widower for more than forty years. Only one of his six children survived him. At the time of this Will and codicil his immediate family was composed of one daughter, a bankrupt son-in-law, and grandchildren. Jefferson, who was trained as a lawyer, drafted a Will that provided that his residuary estate be held in trust for the benefit of his daughter and descendants during the life of his son-in-law.

> Considering the insolvent state of the affairs of my friend & son in law Thomas Mann Randolph, and that what will remain of my property will be the only resource against the want in which his family would otherwise be left, it must be his wish, as it is my duty, to guard that resource against all liability for his debts. ...I do hereby devise and bequeath all the residue of my property...in trust...for the sole and separate use of my dear daughter Martha Randolph and her heirs...

Jefferson was aware that the legal effect of placing the property in trust would be to shield it from his son-in-law's many creditors. However, this legal protection was ultimately futile as Jefferson's own insolvent estate was subject to his creditors' claims.

In 1814, facing mounting debts, Jefferson was forced to sell part of his incomparable library to Congress for $23,950, and those books can be found in the Library of Congress today. Jefferson's bequest of his remaining collection of books to the University of Virginia helped establish that institution as one of the premier learning centers in the nation. Jefferson dispensed with a formal inventory of his property for the following reasons: "In consequence of the variety and undescribableness of the articles of property within the house at Monticello, and the difficulty of inventorying and appraising them separately and specifically, and its inutility, I dispense with having them inventoried and appraised..."

Jefferson appointed his grandson, Thomas Jefferson Randolph, as executor of his Will. To his grandson Jefferson gave "my silver watch in preference to the golden one, because of it's superior excellence, my papers of business going of course to him, as my executor, all others of a literary or other character I give to him as of his own property."

Perhaps most touching in Jefferson's Will is his gift of his gold-mounted walking staff of animal horn to his friend and successor president James Madison, as "a token of the cordial and affectionate friendship which for nearly now an half century has united us in the same principles and pursuits of what we have deemed for the greatest good of our country."

/S/ Thomas Jefferson

WILL DATED: March 16, 1826
Codicil undated
Signed at Monticello in Albemarle County, Virginia

Calvin Coolidge

Date and Place of Birth	Date and Place of Death
July 4, 1972	January 5, 1933
Plymouth, Vermont	Northampton, Massachusetts

Short, and to the Point

Known for his taciturn nature and brevity, Calvin Coolidge had a one-line Will, which is the shortest of any of the presidents', or almost anyone else's. And Coolidge was trained as a lawyer besides!

When he died in 1933, John Calvin Coolidge (as he was named at birth) was survived by his wife, Grace Goodhue Coolidge, and his son, John. As his Will, which he signed in the White House in the middle of his first full term, states:

> Not unmindful of my son John, I give all my estate both real and personal to my wife Grace Coolidge, in fee simple—Home at Washington, District of Columbia this twentieth day of December, A.D. nineteen hundred and twenty six.

By expressly mentioning son John in his Will, Coolidge evidenced that he did not forget to include his son, but purposely intended to leave his entire estate to his wife. We can only speculate as to why Coolidge deliberately disinherited John. Mrs. Coolidge lived until July 8, 1957.

Also known for being thrifty, Coolidge died with an estate

reportedly worth more than $500,000, which was in part derived from his $75,000 annual salary as president.

/S/ Calvin Coolidge

WILL DATED: December 20, 1926
Will signed at the White House, Washington, D.C.

$\mathcal{F}$ranklin $\mathcal{D}$. $\mathcal{R}$oosevelt

Date and Place of Birth	Date and Place of Death
January 30, 1882 Hyde Park, New York	April 12, 1945 "Little White House" Warm Springs, Georgia

$\mathcal{W}$arm $\mathcal{S}$prings $\mathcal{E}$ternal

$\mathcal{W}$hen he died during his unprecedented fourth term as president of the United States, Franklin Roosevelt was survived by five adult children and his wife, Eleanor Roosevelt. Eleanor Roosevelt survived her husband by another seventeen years, dying in 1962.

Roosevelt's Will makes meticulous provisions for the disposition of his tangible personal property among his wife and descendants. For example, there is the following provision pertaining to Eleanor's use of certain tangible property:

> If my wife, ANNA ELEANOR ROOSEVELT shall survive me, I direct that she shall have the right to use during her lifetime, at such place or places as she may wish, all or any part of the jewelry, books, paintings, pictures, works of art, statuary, silver, plate, china, glass, ornaments, rugs, tapestry, automobiles and boats and their equipment, household furniture and equipment and other tangible personal property of a similar kind of nature which I may own at the time of my death and wherever located, except such personal property bequeathed to Georgia Warm Springs Foundation under Article FIFTH of this Will; PROVIDED, HOWEVER, that my said wife shall select the articles of personal prop-

erty to be used by her as aforesaid and shall notify my
Executors in writing of the articles so selected by her
within six (6) months after my death. Upon the receipt
of such written notification by my Executors, my said
wife may take possession of the articles of personal
property so selected by her.

The Will provides lengthy and detailed mechanisms for the
selection of various articles of tangible personal property by
other Roosevelt family members after Eleanor's death.

The natural mineral springs and property located in Warm
Springs, Georgia, were used by Roosevelt to give him some
relief from his affliction by the crippling disease polio. In 1927,
Roosevelt had incorporated the Georgia Warm Springs Foundation as a not-for-profit medical and healing foundation. Under his Will, Roosevelt devised and bequeathed to the Georgia
Warm Springs Foundation all of the real estate, buildings,
and personal property owned by him in Meriwether County,
Georgia.

The bulk of Roosevelt's substantial estate was directed to
be held in trust for the benefit of his wife, Eleanor, and to a
lesser degree for the benefit of his secretary, Marguerite A.
Le Hand. Roosevelt's son James and two attorneys were
named as the executors and trustees of his Will.

The Will directs that Roosevelt's executors "erect a simple
stone over the grave of my wife and myself to be located in
the garden of my property in the Town of Hyde Park, County
of Dutchess and State of New York." Furthermore, Roosevelt
made a $5,000 bequest to the rector, wardens, and vestry of
St. James Church in Hyde Park "to be added to the Cemetery
Fund and used for the upkeep of the Roosevelt family burial
lots, the grave of my wife and myself, and for general cemetery
upkeep purposes."

Finally, as is appropriate for the man who introduced the
New Deal to America, Roosevelt provides the following bequests:

> I give and bequeath to each of the persons who are my
> employees or servants at the time of my death and
> whose salaries or wages are at that time being paid by
> me personally the sum of One Hundred Dollars
> ($100.00).

It is important that the Will limited payment to employees
whose salaries were personally paid by Roosevelt; otherwise,
all United States government workers might have asserted
claims as $100 beneficiaries of their deceased leader's estate.

/S/ *Franklin D. Roosevelt*

WILL DATED: November 12, 1941

Harry Truman

Date and Place of Birth	Date and Place of Death
May 8, 1884 Lamar, Missouri	December 26, 1972 Independence, Missouri

The Buck Stopped in Independence

When he died at the age of eighty-eight, Harry Truman was survived by his wife, Elizabeth "Bess" Truman, who was then eighty-seven years old, his daughter, Margaret, and four grandsons. Harry Truman was also survived by his eighty-three-year-old unmarried sister, Miss Mary Jane Truman, who was a patient in the same hospital as her brother on the night he died.

During his life and in his Will, Truman showed an extraordinary concern with the disposition of his presidential papers and other historical materials. His Will and subsequent codicils indicate Truman's obsession with this issue, as shown by the following brief excerpts from Truman's unusually verbose Will:

> I have from time to time during my life given and transferred to the United States of America all of my right, title and interest in, and the possession of, certain papers, historical materials and other property, to be kept in the Harry S. Truman Library in Independence, Missouri, on certain conditions enumerated in correspondence between me and the Administrator of General Services of the United States and the Archivist of the United States.
>
> . . .

II. All of my remaining historical materials, which shall, for the purposes of this Will, include all cartoons, books, portraits, statues, objets d'art, models, pictures and miscellaneous objects or materials having historical or commemorative values, other than those thereof (a) which shall be located at the time of my death in my private residence in Independence, Missouri or in any other private residence which I or my daughter may have at such time, or (b) which shall contain a label or other indication showing a reservation of title in me, or (c) which shall be determined by my Executors in their sole and absolute discretion to be related in whole or in part of the business or personal affairs of myself or any of the members of my family.

In deference to his wife and daughter, Truman also made the following bequests:

I bequeath all of my papers and historical materials not bequeathed to the United States of America pursuant to the provisions of part B of Article THIRD hereof (a) to my wife and my daughter, in equal shares.

...

TENTH: If my wife shall survive me, and if any (or all) of my daughter and her issue shall also survive me, I devise and bequeath to my wife one-half of the Balance of my Remaining Estate. I direct that said one-half of the Balance of my Remaining Estate shall include the following property:

A. All of my jewelry, clothing and personal effects.

B. Any automobiles which I shall own at the time of my death.

C. All of the household furniture, furnishings and equipment, rugs, silverware, plated ware, china, glassware, linens, books, paintings, pictures and objets d'art which I shall own at the time of my death, other than the property referred to in part B of Article THIRD hereof and in Article SIXTH hereof.

D. All farm machinery and equipment, <u>gardeners'</u>, <u>mechanics' and other tools and domestic animals</u> <u>which I shall own at the time of my death.</u> [emphasis added]

Truman also remembered his local lodge mates with the following devise of real property that he owned:

I devise to Grandview Lodge No. 618, A.F. & A.M., as a site for a Lodge Hall, the southerly one hundred and ten feet of Lots 9 and 10 in Sheltons Addition to Grandview, Missouri.

A number of Bess and Harry Truman's nieces and nephews received bequests of amounts ranging from $5 to $1,000 under Truman's Will:

In addition to the specific bequests made by me in my Will and as above made to the nephews and nieces of myself and Mrs. Bess Wallace Truman, I give and devise to the following greatnephews and greatnieces of myself and my wife the sum of Five Hundred Dollars ($500.00) to each, except to John Ross Truman, I give the sum of Five Dollars ($5.00). They are as follows:

Children of John Curtis Truman:

John Ross Truman	$5.00
Mary Martha Truman	500.00
Rita Marie Truman	500.00
Loretta Ann Truman	500.00
Gilbert Higbee Truman	500.00
Jean Ellen Truman	500.00

It might appear that Truman's grandnephew, John Ross Truman, was disliked by the late president because he receives only a minimal $5 bequest rather than the $500 bequests received by his siblings. It has been reported that this small bequest was attributable to the fact that John Ross Truman was planning to become a Catholic priest in an order that necessitated a vow of poverty. Apparently, practical and thrifty testator Truman determined that it would be pointless to give that particular grandnephew a gift that he would not be able to enjoy directly, but nonetheless remembers him in his Will with a token amount.

Truman's Will also provides the following detailed instructions regarding his burial, gravesite, the "slab over the graves" and the suggested obelisk:

> It is my will and desire, and I direct that my Executrix or Executor arrange and cause my remains to be laid to rest in the center of the plaza South of my office on the premises of THE HARRY S. TRUMAN LIBRARY, in Independence, Missouri.... If it is desired that an obelisk should be put at the head of the graves, and the Executrix or Executor shall so decide. It is my desire that a slab be placed over the graves, whether the obelisk is set up or not.
>
> I would suggest that the slab over the graves, which will lie flat, have the following inscriptions:
>
> HARRY S. TRUMAN
> Born May 8, 1884
> Lamar, Missouri
> Married June 28, 1919
> Daughter Born February 17, 1924
> County Judge Eastern District
> Jackson County
> January 1, 1925
> Presiding Judge, Jackson County

January 1, 1927–January 1, 1935
United States Senator, Missouri
January 3, 1935–January 12, 1945
Vice-President, United States
January 20, to April 12, 1945
President, United States
April 12, 1945–January 20, 1953

Truman's lengthy Will is unusual in including the text of suggested epitaphs for himself and his wife. Pursuant to his wishes, Truman's funeral was privately held in his hometown of Independence, Missouri, and he was buried on the grounds of his beloved Harry S. Truman Library. Harry's buck finally stopped in Independence, Missouri.

/S/ *Harry S. Truman*

WILL DATED: January 14, 1959
FIRST CODICIL DATED: October 23, 1961
SECOND CODICIL DATED: November 4, 1967

John F. Kennedy

Date and Place of Birth	Date and Place of death
May 29, 1917 Brookline, Massachusetts	November 22, 1963 Dallas, Texas

"Mindful of the Uncertainty of Life"

In 1954, the year he signed his last Will and testament, thirty-seven-year-old John F. Kennedy was serving in his first term as a United States senator from Massachusetts. Six years later, the youngest U.S. president would be succeeding the oldest, and Kennedy would be moving his wife, Jacqueline, and young children, Caroline and John, Jr., into the White House. Unfortunately, the Kennedy family's stay in the White House would be short-lived as a result of the tragic assassination of JFK in November 1963. Ironically, the preamble to Kennedy's Will is archaic yet prophetic by his reference to being "mindful of the uncertainty of life."

Kennedy signed this Will before either of his children were born (or the infant death of a third child while in the White House) and certainly before any thought had been given to the disposition of "presidential papers." The Will established trust vehicles to provide primarily for his wife, Jackie, and for any future descendants. In addition, there is the following cash and specific bequest for Jackie:

> I give and bequeath unto my wife, JACQUELINE B. KENNEDY, if she survives me, the sum of Twenty-Five Thousand ($25,000.00) Dollars, together with all of my personal effects, furniture, furnishings, silverware,

147

> dishes, china, glassware and linens, which I may own
> at the time of my death.

As president, Kennedy received an annual salary of $100,000, in addition to a $50,000 expense account. Furthermore, Kennedy was independently wealthy, being the beneficiary of a significant trust fund (reportedly generating annual income in excess of $500,000 per year) from the substantial estate of his father, Joseph P. Kennedy, with the fortune made through shrewd investments and allegedly from bootlegging during Prohibition.

Early in the Will there is a reference to the charitable foundation established in memory of Kennedy's predeceased brother, Joseph P. Kennedy, Jr., who had been young John's primary rival for family and political attention. The provision does not make any gift, but merely refers to prior gifts made. What a politician Kennedy was, even in his Will:

> During my life, I have made substantial contributions
> to divers charities, causes and institutions of all faiths,
> both individually and through The Joseph P. Kennedy
> Jr. Foundation, which was established in honor of my
> late beloved brother. I am certain that the contributions
> which I and other members of my family have made to
> the Foundation will be applied after my death without
> bias or discrimination to the fulfillment of the Foundation's eleemosynary purposes.

Kennedy names his wife and brothers, Robert F. Kennedy and Edward M. Kennedy, to be the executors of his Will. If any of them were unable to serve as an executor, then the vacancy was to be filled by Kennedy's sisters, Eunice K. Shriver, Patricia Lawford, and Jean Kennedy, *in the order named* according to the Will.

It strikes one as unusual that Kennedy did not update his Will after becoming president and entering the White House.

His failure to address presidential issues such as establishing archives for his presidential papers left this issue open for his family and various governmental entities to determine. Nonetheless, the Kennedy legacy has been great, as evidenced by monuments all over the world to the president who won America's heart.

/S/ *John F. Kennedy*

WILL DATED: June 18, 1954
Will signed in Washington, D.C.

THE WRITERS

Last Writes

The Writer	Date of Death
Mark Twain "The Reports of My Death Are Greatly Exaggerated"	April 21, 1910
F. Scott Fitzgerald The Other Side of Paradise	December 21, 1940
William Faulkner As He Lay Dying	July 6, 1962
Tennessee Williams Here Today, Iguana Tomorrow	February 25, 1983
Truman Capote Unfinished Prayers	August 25, 1984
Lillian Hellman Banned in Boston, Dead in the Vineyard	June 30, 1984
James Beard Just Desserts	January 23, 1985

Mark Twain

Date and Place of Birth

November 30, 1835
Florida, Missouri

Date and Place of Death

April 21, 1910
Stormfield
Redding, Connecticut

"The Reports of My Death Are Greatly Exaggerated"

*N*amed Samuel Langhorne Clemens at his birth in Missouri, he took his nom de plume of "Mark Twain" from the expression used by Mississippi River boatmen to describe a certain depth of the water. With his pen name picked, Twain wrote about life on the Mississippi or on other bodies of water, as in his first famous book, *Innocents Abroad*, about his adventures on a steamship bound for the Holy Land.

It was on this trip to the Holy Land that Clemens met Judge Jervis J. Langdon of Elmira, New York, and his daughter Lizzie, who would subsequently become Clemens's wife. Together Clemens and his wife had three daughters and one son. The son died in infancy and one daughter died in her teens. Clemens's wife died during their marriage, and Clemens never remarried. In the year before he died, Clemens's daughter Miss Jean Clemens drowned in the bathtub in her father's house in Redding, Connecticut, on Christmas morning. Despondent over the loss of his daughter, Clemens's own health deteriorated rapidly after her death.

Clemens signed his Will on August 17, 1909, before his daughter Jean died, and he never updated his Will to reflect her death. The Will provides that his daughters Jean and Clara

153

were each to receive 5 percent "of any and all moneys which at the time of my death may be on deposit to my credit, and subject to withdrawal on demand in any bank or trust company, or in any banking institution." The balance of his estate was to be held in trust for his two daughters and their descendants. Since daughter Jean died without any descendants, the entire estate was inherited by Clara, who was married to a man named Ossip Gabrilowitsch.

For his executors and trustees, Clemens named his nephew, Jervis Langdon, and two other "friends" from the city of New York. "Reposing confidence in their integrity," Clemens directed that they should not be required to furnish any bond. Clemens was well aware of the value of his tremendous literary output and included the following provision in his Will related to that:

As I have expressed to my daughter, CLARA LANGDON CLEMENS, and to my associate, ALBERT BIGELOW PAINE, my ideas and desires regarding the administration of my literary productions, and as they are especially familiar with my wishes in that respect, I request that my executors and trustees above named confer and advise with my said daughter CLARA LANGDON CLEMENS, and the said ALBERT BIGELOW PAINE, as to all matters relating in any way to the control, management and disposition of my literary productions, published and unpublished, and all my literary articles and memoranda of every kind and description, and generally as to all matters which pertain to copyrights and such other literary property as I may leave at the time of my decease. The foregoing suggestion as to consultation is, however, made subject to my contract dated July 24th, 1909, with ALBERT BIGELOW PAINE for the preparation of my letters for publication, and in full recognition thereof, and subject also to the contract dated August 27th, 1906, made by and between the said ALBERT BI-

GELOW PAINE and HARPER & BROTHERS, as I have
appointed the said ALBERT BIGELOW PAINE as my
biographer, and have ratified and approved his said contract relating to the publication thereof.

Obviously, Paine was someone whom Clemens trusted and
was also one of the witnesses to Clemens's Will.

A prankster for much of his life, Clemens had once arranged
for his obituary to be printed in New York newspapers. After
the article had appeared Clemens cabled from London the
following famous line: "The reports of my death are greatly
exaggerated." When he did finally succumb to death in his
seventh-fifth year, Clemens is reported to have died quietly
while in an unconscious state and the State of Connecticut.
Earlier that afternoon Clemens had written a note to his
nurses—"Give me my glasses"—because he had been too
weak to speak. On the bed when he died was one book he
had particularly admired and was rereading—Thomas Car-
lyle's *French Revolution*. At his bedside watching the great
writer slip out of this world were his daughter Clara, her
husband Ossip, and Twain's designated biographer, Albert
Bigelow Paine. The reports of Samuel Clemens's/Mark
Twain's death in 1910 in newspapers all across America were
detailed, but not exaggerated.

/S/ *Samuel L. Clemens*

WILL DATED: August 17, 1909

F. Scott Fitzgerald

Date and Place of Birth	Date and Place of Death
September 24, 1896 St. Paul, Minnesota	December 21, 1940 Hollywood, California

The Other Side of Paradise

Fatally stricken by a heart attack at the age of forty-four, F. Scott Fitzgerald was one of America's leading literary voices during the roaring twenties. He began his first novel, *This Side of Paradise*, in 1916 while still an undergraduate at Princeton University. In 1917 he left Princeton, ostensibly to join the Army and fight for his country, but also as a result of failing grades. While stationed in Alabama, he met and married Zelda Sayre, who has been called "the brilliant counterpart" of the heroines in his novels. In 1921, F. Scott and Zelda had their only child, Frances Scott Fitzgerald. F. Scott published his most famous novel, *The Great Gatsby*, in 1925 "at a time when gin was the national drink and sex the national obsession," according to his obituary in *The New York Times*. During the last years of his life, Fitzgerald's literary output was minimal, and many have claimed that his early promise of a brilliant career was never fulfilled as a result of alcoholism and other personal problems.

Fitzgerald's handwritten Will appears to have been written without the assistance of an attorney, while Fitzgerald was in North Carolina "drying out" late in his life. It is interesting to note the unusual preamble to the Will, which speaks of "the uncertainty of life *and the certainty of death*" [emphasis added].

Three years after signing the Will, Fitzgerald made some

revealing changes to it pertaining to his own burial. On November 10, 1940, less than two months before his death, Fitzgerald made the following change:

> ITEM ONE: I will and direct that at my death my executors to be hereinafter named shall provide for me ~~a suitable~~ the cheapest funeral and burial ~~in keeping with my station in life and in due regard to the bequests hereinafter made~~, the same to be without any undue ostentation and unnecessary expense.

F. Scott Fitzgerald, Nov. 10th, 1940

Perhaps most unusual about this Will are Fitzgerald's repeated references to his wife's, Zelda's, insanity. Early in the Will, Fitzgerald states that Zelda is "non Compos Mentis" (Latin for "not sound of mind; insane"). Subsequently, the Will provides:

> ITEM SIX: I give, devise and bequeath unto my wife, Zelda Fitzgerald in the event she shall regain her sanity all of my household and kitchen furniture to be used and controlled by her as she may desire...
> ITEM SEVEN: In the event that my wife has not regained her sanity at my death, I give, devise and bequeath unto my said daughter, Frances Scott Fitzgerald, the above designated household and kitchen furniture to be held by her for Zelda Fitzgerald during her lifetime or until she shall regain her sanity....
> ITEM EIGHT: I give, devise and bequeath unto my daughter, Frances Scott Fitzgerald all my family silverware, portraits, pictures, and all special and valuable books, short stories or other writings which I may have written, or all books of value which I may have collected or purchased to be used and controlled by her until my wife Zelda Fitzgerald shall regain her sanity...

It is revealing that Fitzgerald's Will never provides who would make the determination whether Zelda had regained her sanity or not. Perhaps that omission is an indication that Fitzgerald did not believe that his wife would ever regain her sanity.

Fitzgerald's only daughter, Frances, was attending Vassar College when he died in 1940. Zelda Fitzgerald lived eight years more and died on March 11, 1948. Upon Zelda's death, the balance of the estate, including all Fitzgerald's literary-property interests, passed entirely to the Fitzgeralds' only child, Frances.

/S/ F. Scott Fitzgerald

DATE OF WILL: June 17, 1937
PLACE OF WILL SIGNING: Polk County, North Carolina
DATE OF WILL CHANGES: November 10, 1940

William Faulkner

Date and Place of Birth	Date and Place of Death
September 25, 1897 New Albany, Mississippi	July 6, 1962 Oxford, Mississippi

As He Lay Dying

Born and bred in Mississippi, Nobel and Pulitzer Prize–winning author William Faulkner introduced the entire world to *his* world of fictional Yoknapatawpha County, Mississippi. According to Faulkner, "Yoknapatawpha" was a Chickasaw Indian term meaning "water passes slowly through the flatlands," and the fictional place in his novels was modeled on his own home county of Lafayette, Mississippi.

Besides his literary brilliance, Faulkner was an indefatigable horseman and a bona fide bourbon-sipping southern gentleman. One day while riding on his farm in old Miss, a horse bucked him, and that buck indirectly led to his death. Nonetheless, he was drinking his bourbon "as a painkiller" until shortly before his end. A painkiller it was, indeed.

In his Will, Faulkner ("being the same person as William Falkner, of Charlottesville, Virginia") named his daughter, Jill Faulkner Summers, as his sole executor and trustee of the trust for the benefit of his wife, Estelle Oldham Faulkner, whom Faulkner had married in 1929. Mrs. Faulkner receives approximately one-half of her husband's estate in trust, with the balance of the estate being paid outright to Faulkner's daughter, Jill.

Faulkner makes two $5,000 bequests, to a niece and a nephew, but for the most part, his Will is rather technical and dry, and disappointing for anyone hoping to see Faulkner's vernacular style showing through. There is no reference of any kind to Faulkner's tremendous literary output.

For several years before his death Faulkner was an enigmatic presence on the University of Virginia campus. In a codicil signed in December of 1960, Faulkner gives to The William Faulkner Foundation, Charlottesville, Virginia, "all of my manuscripts and other tangible personal property deposited at the Alderman Library of the University of Virginia."

/S/ William Faulkner

WILL DATED: June 1, 1960
CODICIL DATED: December 28, 1960
Residing in Charlottesville, Virginia

Tennessee Williams

Date and Place of Birth	Date and Place of Death
March 26, 1911	February 25, 1983
Columbus, Mississippi	Hotel Élysée
	New York, New York

Here Today, Iguana Tomorrow

Playwright Tennessee Williams's prodigious output created some of the English-speaking theater's most riveting dramas, including *Cat on a Hot Tin Roof*, *A Streetcar Named Desire*, and *The Night of the Iguana*. Despite his repeated critical successes, Williams was known to be sensitive about criticism of, or changes to, his writings. In his Will, Williams gives explicit directions that none of his literary works should be altered, stating:

> It is my wish that no play which I shall have written shall, for the purpose of presenting it as a first-class attraction on the English-speaking stage, be changed in any manner, whether such change shall be by way of completing it, or adding to it, or deleting from it, or in any other way revising it, except for the customary type of stage directions. It is also my wish and will that no poem or literary work of mine be changed in any manner, whether such change shall be by way of completing any such work or adding to it or deleting from it or in any other way revising it, except that any complete poem or other literary work of mine may be translated into a foreign language or dramatized for stage, screen or television. I expressly direct that neither my

Executors nor my Trustees make or authorize the making of any changes prohibited in this Article. To the extent that I can legally do so, no party who shall acquire any rights in any play, poem or literary work of mine shall have the right to make or authorize the making of any changes in any play, poem or literary work of mine prohibited in this Article.

When he was born in Mississippi, Williams was named Thomas Lanier Williams. Apparently his childhood was an unhappy one; his father, Cornelius Coffin Williams, was reported to be a violent and brutish traveling salesman. Williams had an older sister named Rose, who had mental problems, and after the failure of a frontal lobotomy operation, Rose spent most of the rest of her life in mental institutions.

After taking nine years to complete his college education, at the age of twenty-eight Williams left home for New Orleans and invented a new name for himself—"Tennessee." It was while living in New Orleans that Williams wrote *A Streetcar Named Desire*. At the time of his death, Williams reportedly still maintained an apartment in the French Quarter of New Orleans in addition to his home in Key West, Florida, and a suite at the Hotel Élysée in New York.

At the time he signed his Will in 1980, Williams was working on a play tentatively titled *Two Character Play*. The name of that play was finally changed to *Out Cry*. Under the first article of his Will Williams gives all the royalties and other proceeds from that play to "my good friend, LADY MARIA ST. JUST of London, England." Unfortunately for Lady Just, this Williams play has not been a commercial success.

In his 1980 Will, Williams directed that many of his personal journals, diaries, and other literary properties should either be sold or given to the University of the South. However, in a codicil to his Will, which Williams signed in 1982, he changed the recipient of his valuable papers from the University of the South to Harvard University.

Most of Williams's estate was placed in trust for the benefit of his mentally deranged sister, Rose, who lived at the Stony Lodge Sanitarium in Ossining, New York. Expressing the wish that the trustees provide liberally for his sister, Williams's Will states:

> In addition to the payment of the normal expenses of maintenance of said Institution, my Trustees shall pay ...such amounts as they deem necessary or advisable for medical and dental expenses, clothing and her usual customary pleasures as she now enjoys, including shopping trips to New York City, personal spending money, it being my intention that said Trustees shall provide liberally for her, not only for her needs but also for her comfort and pleasures.

In addition to providing for his sister, Williams's Will provides that his brother, Walter Dakin Williams, is to receive a lump-sum payment of $25,000 upon Rose's death. "I have intentionally made no other provision for my said brother as he is well provided for."

The rest of the property remaining after Rose's death was originally to be paid to the University of the South, but that bequest was also changed to Harvard University. Williams directs that that property is to be held in a separate fund called the "WALTER E. DAKIN MEMORIAL FUND" to be used for "the purposes of encouraging creative writing and creative writers in need of financial assistance to pursue their vocation whose work is progressive, original and preferably of an experimental nature."

It was in his suite at the Hotel Élysée that Tennessee Williams was found dead on the morning of February 25, 1983, by his secretary. According to the chief medical examiner's report, Williams choked to death on a bottle cap that had become lodged in his larynx. Williams's inability to gag and expel the object lodged in his throat was possibly attributable to impaired response caused by the presence of drugs and/or alcohol. According to police reports, an empty bottle of wine and several types of medication were found in the room where Williams died. Mr. Williams's history with alcohol and drugs was well-known and may have been the silent cause of his death. Choking to death on a bottle cap, brilliant playwright Tennessee Williams unbottled human emotions and expressed those emotions by words uttered by characters of his imagination.

/S/ Tennessee Williams

WILL DATED: September 11, 1980
CODICIL DATED: December 1982

Truman Capote

Date and Place of Birth	Date and Place of Death
September 30, 1924 New Orleans, Louisiana	August 25, 1984 Bel Air, California (Joanna Carson's home)

Unfinished Prayers

Truman Capote, a self-proclaimed homosexual, provided in his Will primarily for his longtime companion, "my friend, JOHN PAUL DUNPHY." Under the Will, Dunphy was to receive all real estate owned by Capote at his death. At the time of his death, Capote owned an apartment at the United Nations Plaza in New York and an apartment in Verbier, Switzerland.

To dispose of Capote's tangible personal property, the Will provides under the first article:

> I give so much of my tangible personal property to such persons (including himself) as my Executor [Alan U. Schwartz] determines that I would wish to receive such property. I give the balance of my tangible personal property to my friend, JOHN PAUL DUNPHY, if he survives me.

This provision gave Capote's attorney, Alan U. Schwartz, unusually broad discretion to dispose of Capote's most personal property, including manuscripts, books, objects of art collected by Capote, and other items of potentially significant value. Rather than making the decisions pertaining to the disposition of this property himself, Capote shifted those decisions to Schwartz. The ultimate disposition of this property is not a matter of public record, and we can only wonder what John Paul Dunphy's (and other Capote friends') share of the property was.

According to papers filed with the New York Surrogate's Court, Capote's estate was worth well in excess of $2 million when he died. The bulk of the estate was to be placed in trust for the benefit of John Paul Dunphy until his death. Upon the death of Dunphy, the property remaining in the trust is to be held by a charitable trust with the following purpose:

> My Trustee shall pay the income from the trust to a college or university located in the United States that will agree to establish a prize or prizes to be awarded annually for excellence in literary criticism. The prize shall be known as the Truman Capote award for Literary Criticism in memory of Newton Arvin. My trustee is authorized to allow a reasonable portion of the funds to be used by the college or university to administer the award. The prizes shall be awarded on a competitive basis in a manner similar to awarding of the Pulitzer Prize... I authorize my trustee to pay the trust income annually or more frequently to one or more colleges or universities located in the United States to provide scholarships for promising writers.

Newton Arvin, in whose memory the Capote award for literary criticism is established, was one of Capote's most influential lovers and his literary mentor. Arvin was a professor of English literature at the all-women Smith College when Capote met him in the summer of '46. A most learned man, Arvin read French, German, Italian, Latin, and of course, Greek. Besides their sexual/romantic liaisons, Arvin became the college professor that the self-taught and somewhat provincial Truman Capote never had. Arvin died of cancer in 1963. His impact on Capote was crucial to Capote's literary development. It seems fitting that in the Will Capote signed almost twenty years after Arvin's death, he would honor his former lover, mentor, and literary Virgil by naming the award for literary criticism in his memory.

Named Truman Streckfus Persons at his birth in New Orleans, Louisiana, Truman later adopted the surname of his mother's second husband, Joe Capote. His mother was an alcoholic and eventually committed suicide. Capote's younger years were spent being shuttled among relatives throughout the South. Capote later worked at *The New Yorker* and displayed great precociousness as a writer; his first published book, *Other Voices, Other Rooms,* appearing when he was twenty-three, established him as a young writer whose star was rising. Capote wrote intermittently throughout the 1950s, 1960s, and 1970s, including the popular *Breakfast at Tiffany's.* However, it was his searing "nonfiction novel," *In Cold Blood,* about the cold-blooded murder of the Herbert Clutter family in rural Kansas and the mentality, trial, and execution of the Clutter killers, that shocked and captivated America.

Capote continued writing until his death, but much of it was gossip about the celebrities whom he had courted. He became addicted to alcohol and drugs and proclaimed to the world in a 1980 interview, "I'm an alcoholic. I'm a drug addict. I'm homosexual. I'm a genius. Of course, I could be all four of those dubious things and still be a saint." At the time of his alleged overdose from sleeping pills in the home of Joanna Carson, Capote was working on "his masterwork," entitled *Answered Prayers.* For Truman Capote, those prayers were never finished.

/S/ *Truman Capote*

Signed at Apt 22G, U.N. Plaza, N.Y.—Capote's apartment
DATE SIGNED: May 4, 1981

Lillian Hellman

Date and Place of Birth	Date and Place of Death
June 20, 1905 New Orleans, Louisiana	June 30, 1984 Martha's Vineyard, Massachusetts

Banned in Boston, Dead in the Vineyard

Best known for her scandalous 1934 play entitled *The Children's Hour,* which was banned in Boston, Chicago, and other cities, Lillian Hellman was controversial throughout her life until her death at the age of seventy-nine.

Her most well-known alliance was to writer Dashiell Hammett, with whom she lived off and on for over thirty years until his death in 1960. In her 1984 Will Hellman makes several references to her former lover Hammett, including the following bequest:

> I give and bequeath all my right, title and interest in and to the works of Dashiell Hammett or works based upon his writings (including, but not limited to, books, stories, plays, scripts and theatrical, radio, movie or television productions) to the fiduciaries hereinafter named, IN TRUST... I further request that the fiduciaries in making such selections shall be guided by the political, social and economic beliefs which, of course, were radical, of the late Dashiell Hammett who was a believer in the doctrines of Karl Marx.

As trustees of the Dashiell Hammett Fund, Hellman named John Hersey, Jules Feiffer, Ephraim London, Howard Bay, and Isadore Englander.

As for her own literary property, Hellman gave all her "original writings, manuscripts, papers, notes, memoranda and other literary property," excluding a manuscript to be selected by her friend Mike Nichols, to the University of Texas in Austin.

At the time of her death, Ms. Hellman was not married and had no children. However, she did have quite a collection of friends and admirers (despite some harsh critics) and had also collected many objects of sentimental value, which she designated for particular friends. The following list of bequests reads like a literary who's who and gives a good indication of Hellman's various relationships.

I give and bequeath the following articles of my tangible personal property except cash, wherever located, to such of the persons hereinafter named as shall survive me:

(1) to BLAIR CLARK, the English or American Hiboy chest in the bedroom of my New York apartment and any photographs of me he may choose, except the one effectively bequeathed in item "(12)" hereof.

(2) to MIKE NICHOLS, the Toulouse Lautrec poster in the hall of my New York apartment, any of the manuscripts in my possession and the Italian sconces in the hall of my apartment.

(3) to ANNABEL NICHOLS, my diamond necklace recently made from a bracelet.

(4) to RITA WADE, any and all coats she may choose; my gold watch and large platinum diamond pin, feather design; the Betamax in the study of my New York apartment and any other object she may choose, except as otherwise designated;

(5) to BARBARA HERSEY and JOHN HERSEY, or to BROOK HERSEY, the Queen Anne table in the living room of my Martha's Vineyard house; to BARBARA

HERSEY, the platinum flower diamond pin; and any other piece of furniture and any and all paintings or pictures that JOHN HERSEY may choose from either my Martha's Vineyard house or my New York apartment, except as otherwise designated.

(6) to SELMA WOLFMAN, the pallet pin which Dashiell Hammett gave to me.

(7) to MAX PALEVSKY, the Spanish table presently in the study of my New York apartment; ... the framed Russian altar cloth presently over the fireplace in the living room, given to me by Pudovkin, the movie director, as it was executed by a member of his family in 1796; any pictures or statues of art work that he may choose, except as otherwise designated; and the two chairs against the wall near the sofa in the living room of my New York apartment, made by unknown cabinet makers in Bohemia or possibly France and exchanged by these amateurs one to the other in the early nineteenth century; and any other object he may choose, except as otherwise designated.

(8) to RICHARD POIRIER, any and all books he may choose; the three-step library ladder in the study of my New York apartment; the three (3) Russian china doves, the French secretary and two electrified brass lamps with tulip bulbs in the living room of my New York apartment; and the rare 18th century Bibilo bookcase in the bedroom of my New York apartment.

(9) to DR. GEORGE GERO, all the Russian icons he may choose, except as otherwise designated.

(10) to HOWARD BAY, the Forain drawing and the wooden birdcage hanging from the ceiling in the living room of my New York apartment.

(11) to RICHARD De COMBRAY, the small empire French loveseat and the four Empire arm chairs in the living room of my New York apartment; the four-

pronged French candlesticks on my bedroom fireplace;
and the English wall sconces near the fireplace on my
living room wall and the chandeliers in my bedroom.

(12) to DR. MARTIN WEXLER (of Los Angeles, California), the Ben Shahn portrait of Albert Einstein and
the enlarged photograph of me as a child with nurse,
and the two (2) pictures depicting the ages of man, and
any other object he may choose, except as otherwise
designated.

(13) to JOHN MARQUAND, the small blue dial Cartier
clock that was given to me by his wife, Sue Marquand.

(14) to MILDRED LOFTUS, the 18th century silver
set with pistol handle knives, forks, spoons, etc. from
Chichton in London.

(15) to JOSEPH WEINSTEIN and MRS. JOSEPH
("BOBBIE") WEINSTEIN, the special bound gift copies
of my plays and books given me by Arthur Thornhill.

(16) to WILLIAM ABRAHAMS, the box in the guest
bathroom of my New York apartment that has the little
foxes on it; and any other object he may choose, except
as otherwise designated.

(17) to EPHRAIM LONDON, the Rouault in the living
room of my New York apartment; and any other object
he may choose except as otherwise designated.

(18) The balance of my tangible personal property
including any items not hereinbefore effectively disposed of, shall be dealt with and disposed of as follows:

a) to PETER FEIBLEMAN, any ten (10) items
thereof that he may choose; and fifty (50%) percent
of all royalties due or to become due for my literary
work only, and upon his death, all royalties shall be
paid to the Lillian Hellman Fund.

b) The remainder of such balance in as nearly equal
shares as practicable to JACK H. KLEIN, LORD VIC-
TOR PRITCHETT and LADY DOROTHY PRITCHETT,

JOHN MELBY, FRED GARDNER, RUTH FIELD, JASON EPSTEIN, WILLIAM ABRAHAMS and ANNABEL NI-CHOLS.

At the time of her death Hellman was romantically linked with Peter Feibleman. In addition to the bequest mentioned above, Feibleman received $100,000 outright, the right to use and occupy Hellman's property in Vineyard Haven on Martha's Vineyard for the rest of his life, and the option to buy her New York apartment on Park Avenue at its appraised value. The Will also makes monetary bequests to other friends, including a $35,000 bequest to each of the grandchildren of Dashiell Hammett "to be designated as a gift from Dashiell Hammett."

The rest of Hellman's substantial estate, including her interest in Hammett's estate, was to be held in trust in two separate funds: "The Lillian Hellman Fund" and "The Dashiell Hammett Fund." The Hellman fund was to make grants or gifts "to any person to assist him or her in engaging in writing in any field or upon any subject, or in scientific research, anywhere in the world . . . gifts or grants shall be made from the general public, with preference given to persons showing distinction or promise in writing, but without regard to race, creed, national origin, age, sex or political beliefs." The Hammett fund was intended to "make gifts or grants for the promotion and advancement of political, social and economic equality, civil rights and civil liberties to any person, cause or organization, anywhere in the world, but preferably here in the United States. . . . I further request that the fiduciaries in making such selections shall be guided by the political, social and economic beliefs which, of course, were radical, of the late Dashiell Hammett who was a believer in the doctrines of Karl Marx." One wonders whether in 1984, twenty-four years after his death, the "late" Dashiell Hammett would still have been a believer in the political ideology of Karl Marx.

In her Will, Hellman also made a $2,500 bequest to Temple Israel of New York City as a fund for the perpetual care of the cemetery plot of her parents in Hastings-on-Hudson, New York. For her own burial, she provided that her executors purchase a cemetery plot and "suitable tombstone" and that she be buried in the Chilmark section of Martha's Vineyard. One month and five days after she signed her Will, Lillian Hellman died of a cardiac arrest in her summer home in Martha's Vineyard.

Even after her death, Hellman was the source of controversy. Her Will, though seemingly carefully prepared by her attorneys, was seriously flawed. For one thing, she named certain persons as her "literary property fiduciaries," but never established any literary property trust under the Will. As New York County Surrogate Marie Lambert wrote in her decision in the construction proceeding brought to interpret the Will, "while [Lillian Hellman's] literary works can be characterized as creative genius, her Will cannot."

/S/ *Lillian Hellman*

WILL DATED: May 25, 1984

James Beard

Date and Place of Birth	Date and Place of Death
May 5, 1903 Portland, Oregon	January 23, 1985 New York Hospital New York, New York

Just Desserts

Chef and prolific cookbook writer James Andrew Beard's own physical appearance betrayed his fascination with food; he reportedly weighed over 275 pounds throughout most of his adult life. In an obituary in *The New York Times*, fellow food connoisseur Craig Claiborne described Beard as "a giant panda, Santa Claus and the Jolly Green Giant rolled into one" and added that Beard "wore his rotundity with dignity and grace."

At the outset, Beard's Will proclaims, "I declare that I am not married and have no children." The bulk of his estate, including the New York town house/cooking school that he owned at 167 West 12th Street, New York, New York, Beard left in trust for his "good friend, GINO COFACCI." Upon Cofacci's death the remaining property in the trust was to pass to Beard's alma mater, Reed College in Portland. In addition, the royalties accruing from Beard's numerous cookbooks, including *Beard on Bread, How to Eat Better for Less Money*, and Beard's tour de force, *The Complete Book of Outdoor Cookery*, was to be paid to two named friends for their lifetimes and upon their deaths would revert to Reed College.

Beard died of a cardiac arrest at the age of eighty-one. At the time of his death he was working on another cookbook, entitled *Menus and Memories*. Considering how well and how much he ate and drank during his lifetime, Beard must have had many epicurean memories indeed.

/S/ James A. Beard

WILL DATED: August 13, 1976
CODICIL DATED: June 4, 1983

THE PRODUCERS AND DIRECTORS

No More Lights,
No More Cameras,
No More Action

The Producer or Director	Date of Death
Walt Disney A Mickey Mouse Operation	December 15, 1966
Alfred Hitchcock The Master of Suspense Until the End	April 29, 1980
Lee Strasberg Madness in Monroe's Method	February 17, 1982
Orson Welles Raising Kane	October 10, 1985
Vincente Minnelli Just a Matter of Time	July 25, 1986
John Cassavetes A Man Under the Influence	February 3, 1989

Walt Disney

Date and Place of Birth	Date and Place of Death
December 5, 1901 Chicago, Illinois	December 15, 1966 St. Joseph's Hospital Los Angeles, California

A Mickey Mouse Operation

Walter Elias Disney was raised on a farm. That might partially explain his fascination with mice, ducks, dogs, deer, crickets, pigs, and just about every other kind of animal real or imagined. In his creations of Mickey and Minnie, Donald and Daffy, Pluto, Bambi, Jiminy, and three little pigs, it has been said that Disney was the first person to give animals a soul and imbue them with distinct personalities.

About his most famous international star, known as Topolino in Italy, Michel Souris in France, Miki Kuchi in Japan, Miguel Ratoncito in Spain, and Mikki Maus in Russia, Disney once said, "Sometimes I've tried to figure out why Mickey appealed to the whole world. . . . He's a pretty nice fellow who never does anybody any harm, who gets into scraps through no fault of his own, but always manages to come up grinning. Why, Mickey's even been faithful to one girl, Minnie, all his life. Mickey is so simple and uncomplicated, so easy to understand that you can't help liking him."

Like his favorite character Mickey Mouse, Walt himself was married to one girl all his life. He married the woman who had been the maid of honor at his brother Roy's wedding on April 7, 1925. Lillian Bounds was from Idaho and had been working as an inker and painter at the Disney Studios. On July 13, 1925, Walt married Lillian in her uncle's living room in Idaho. After their marriage, Lillian worked at the studio in times of need and was with her husband over forty years later until the night before he died. Together, they had two daughters, Diane and Sharon. As Walt's 1966 Will states:

> I declare that I am married to LILLIAN B. DISNEY and that I have only two children, namely, DIANE DAISEY MILLER and SHARON DISNEY BROWN.

To Lillian, Disney gave "all of my tangible personal property and personal effects, including without limitation, all my household furniture, furnishings, silverware, books, paintings, works of art, automobiles, clothing, jewelry, miniatures, awards and all other similar items." In addition, Lillian was the beneficiary and a trustee of a family trust consisting of 45 percent of Disney's residuary estate, which was quite substantial and continues to receive royalty payments from the many Disney creations. Another 45 percent of the residuary trust was distributed to the Disney charitable foundation, which contributed part of its funds toward the completion of Disney's esteemed California Institute of the Arts ("Cal Arts") campus. The remaining 10 percent of the residuary estate was held in trust for a group of Disney relatives.

In his Will, Disney appointed his wife, Lillian, his attorney, Herbert F. Sturdy, and the United California Bank as his executors. The Will was prepared by one of Los Angeles's most expensive law firms and is quite detailed.

There is also the standard *in terrorem* clause and the following:

> Except as otherwise provided in this Will, I have intentionally and with full knowledge omitted to provide for my heirs, including any persons who may claim to be an issue of mine.

Perhaps Walt was concerned that there might be some others claiming to be little Disney mice scampering around.

Conspicuously absent from Disney's Will are any instructions or provisions for his funeral or burial. It has been reported that Disney was intrigued by the possibilities of cryogenesis. (Cryogenesis is the scientific technique whereby a person may be chemically frozen or preserved until a cure for the particular fatal ailment has been discovered.) It has long been rumored that Disney himself opted to avail himself of cryogenesis. However, papers filed with the court indicate a payment made by Disney's estate to the Forest Lawn Memorial Park Association in Glendale, California, in an amount exceeding $40,000 "for the interment property, a memorial tablet, Endowment Care Fund deposit and state and city sales taxes." It is noteworthy that the interment property was not selected until September 19, 1967, almost a year after Disney's death. It may have been this delay that has fueled the speculation of Walt Disney on ice.

Seeming to whistle while he worked throughout his productive career, Walt Disney left a legacy of happiness, dopiness, grumpiness, bashfulness, and sheer joyfulness. All around the world, countless wishes have been made on his stars.

/S/ *Walter E. Disney*

WILL DATED: March 18, 1966

Alfred Hitchcock

Date and Place of Birth	**Date and Place of Death**
August 13, 1899	April 29, 1980
London, England	10957 Bellagio Road
	Los Angeles, California

The Master of Suspense Until the End

*A*n undisputed master of suspense, Alfred Hitchcock often turned the world upside down or inside out in his movies. But despite plots filled with international intrigue, suspicion, violence, or sexual obsession, Hitchcock himself appears to have had a stable and serene personal life, especially by Hollywood standards. He married his assistant Alma Reville in 1926, and they remained married for the next fifty-four years until the day he died. Alma worked on many of his films as his general assistant or as a writer. The couple had one child, Patricia, who appeared in several of Hitchcock's films and on his television shows, "Alfred Hitchcock Presents" and the "Alfred Hitchcock Hour," broadcast during the late 1950s and early 1960s.

Like the intricately woven plots that deliberately and methodically unfold in his films, Hitchcock signed his Will in 1963, and then proceeded to make six sets of changes to that Will during the next seventeen years. The last codicil was signed only one month before he died. The signature on that final codicil shows the serious effects that his arthritis had on Hitchcock's ability to sign his name.

Compared to the richness of his cinematic imagery, Hitchcock's twenty-five-page Will is rather dry. Despite the lengthy legal verbiage, there is little of Hitchcock's personality showing through. Not one of his great films is mentioned, nor any particular items from his large collection of art or other memorabilia. Essentially, the entire estate is left to his wife, outright and in trust, with the remainder passing to his daughter and then grandchildren.

Hitchcock's Will is also unusual in that the *in terrorem* clauses appear on page one, rather than being more discreetly placed in the "boilerplate" clauses later in the Will. Despite the prominent placement of this clause in his Will, one wonders whether Hitchcock might have enjoyed a battle royal over his estate.

Also unusual about the Hitchcock Will is that his longtime wife, Alma, signed a "waiver" that was attached to the Will and also admitted to probate. This unusual waiver states in part:

> I, ALMA REVILLE HITCHCOCK, wife of ALFRED J.
> HITCHCOCK, have read the foregoing Will of my husband.... I am fully convinced of the reasonableness and wisdom of the provisions of this Will, and I hereby elect to accept and acquiesce in the provisions of his Will, waiving all claims to my share of any community property and all other claims that I may have upon any of the property disposed of by his Will...

Draw your own conclusions of Hitchcockian intrigue on that one.

As mentioned above, Hitchcock made six subsequent changes to his 1963 Will. Some of these codicils change the changes made in prior codicils, and one wonders why a new Will was not prepared. Perhaps Hitchcock wanted people to see how his thinking had changed over the years. The most significant and startling change is the one he made in the final codicil he signed about one month before he died. In that final codicil, Hitchcock removed his wife, Alma, his friend and previous agent Lew Wasserman, who was then the chairman and chief executive officer of Universal Studios, and an attorney named Citron as his executors and trustees. He retained his longtime attorney Samuel Taylor and added his daughter, Patricia, as a co-executor and co-trustee with Hitch's Taylor. We can only speculate about the reasons for this radical change shortly before Hitchcock died at the age of eighty.

/S/ *Alfred J. Hitchcock*

WILL DATED: August 8, 1963
ALMA HITCHCOCK'S WAIVER DATED: August 8, 1963
FIRST CODICIL DATED: December 7, 1965
SECOND CODICIL DATED: January 30, 1967
THIRD CODICIL DATED: July 3, 1969
FOURTH CODICIL DATED: November 17, 1971
FIFTH CODICIL DATED: August 3, 1977
SIXTH CODICIL DATED: March 25, 1980

Lee Strasberg

Date and Place of Birth	Date and Place of Death
November 17, 1901	February 17, 1982
Budzanow, Poland	New York, New York

Madness in Monroe's Method

When he was born in a town in Poland that is now part of Russia, Strasberg was named Israel Strassberg. When he was seven his family moved to the United States, where Strassberg subsequently Americanized his name to I. Lee Strasberg, and later dropped the "I." As a legendary acting teacher, Lee Strasberg opened the eyes of a generation of American actors, including Marlon Brando, Robert DeNiro, and Marilyn Monroe. Commenting on Strasberg's "method" of acting, Tennessee Williams once said that Strasberg-trained actors are more intense and honest: "They act from the inside out. They communicate emotions they really feel. They give you a sense of life."

During his life, Strasberg apparently had a profound impact on Marilyn Monroe around the time she signed her last Will in 1961. (Monroe's Will is excerpted on page 18 of this volume.) In her Will, Monroe gave Strasberg 75 percent of her residuary estate and all her tangible personal property to dispose of as he deemed appropriate. Ironically, when Strasberg himself died in 1982, he left his entire estate, including his substantial interest in Monroe's estate, to his third wife, Anna. Sixty-seven-year-old Strasberg had married then thirty-one-year-old Anna Mizrahi in 1968, six years after Monroe's death. One wonders whether Monroe would really have wanted

Strasberg's third and final wife to inherit the substantial continuing income from her estate.

Strasberg's first two wives died while married to him. He was survived by his third wife, Anna, and four children—"ADAM and DAVID STRASBERG, sons of my present marriage, and JOHN STRASBERG and SUSAN STRASBERG, children of my first marriage." As mentioned earlier, Strasberg left his entire estate to Anna, but if she had not survived him, the estate was to be left to his two sons from his third marriage, Adam and David. Perhaps Strasberg believed he had already adequately provided for his two older children. It is interesting to note that his daughter, Susan Strasberg, is named as a successor guardian for her stepbrothers, Adam and David, if Anna had not survived.

Ultimately, it would not matter because the then forty-five-year-old Anna survived her eighty-year-old husband and inherited his entire estate, valued at over one and one-half million dollars, plus the lion's share of the Marilyn Monroe legacy as well. Widow Anna Strasberg was subsequently appointed the sole administrator of the Monroe estate by the New York court. With Monroe's estate still generating enormous annual income, Monroe might feel mad that she took some expensive acting lessons from a master of the method.

/S/ *Lee Strasberg*

WILL DATED: April 24, 1981
Residing at 135 Central Park West, New York, New York

Orson Welles

Date and Place of Birth	Date and Place of Death
May 6, 1915 Kenosha, Wisconsin	October 10, 1985 1717 N. Stanley Avenue Los Angeles, California

Raising Kane

Radio broadcaster, actor, and film director Orson Welles was a source of controversy from the time of his faked broadcast of a Martian invasion of New Jersey in 1938 through his tour de force film *Citizen Kane* and until the day he died. Welles's Will was also controversial because it included substantial gifts to a woman who was not Welles's wife.

In his 1982 Will, Welles makes the following bequests and devise of real property to a woman who had been his companion for several years:

> I hereby give to Olga Palinkas (also known as Oja Kodar), whose address is Post Restante Primosten, Republic of Yugoslavia, the house located at 1717 North Stanley Avenue, Los Angeles, California ... and all of the improvements and household furniture, furnishings, pictures, books, silver, paintings, works of art and other personal effects therein.... All taxes attributable to this bequest shall be paid from the residue of my Estate.

Welles left his residuary estate to his third wife, the Italian actress Paola Mori Welles, whom he had married in 1955. If Mrs. Welles had not survived her husband, then Welles's residuary estate was to be left entirely to Olga Palinkas.

To each of his three daughters, Rebecca, Christopher, and

Beatrice, Welles made a $10,000 bequest. Daughter Christopher was the issue of his first marriage, to Virginia Nicholson. Daughter Rebecca was Welles's child with his second wife, Rita Hayworth. And daughter Beatrice was Welles's child with his third and final wife, Paola. Although Welles had been divorced from his first two wives, he treated all his daughters equally under his Will.

As the executor of his Will, Welles named producer Greg Garrison, whom Welles had first met in 1946 and with whom Welles collaborated often in his later years. Apparently, Welles felt that neither his wife Paola nor friend Olga were appropriate for the role of his executor.

Finally, the Will contains this unusual section excerpted from the *in terrorem* clause:

> If any beneficiary under this Will in any manner directly or indirectly contests or attacks this Will or any of its provisions, including paragraph B or Article FOURTH hereof giving the entire house to Olga Palinkas, any share or interest in my Estate given to such beneficiary under this Will is revoked and shall be disposed of in the same manner provided herein as if such beneficiary had predeceased me leaving no living lawful descendants.

By specifically referring to the gift to his companion Olga, Welles obviously wanted to prevent his wife from contesting the gift of his California home to his beautiful companion. Although Welles maintained a home in Los Angeles, California, he was a legal resident of Nevada when he died. It was, however, in his Los Angeles home that Welles suffered the fatal heart attack that killed him.

/S/ *Orson Welles*

WILL DATED: January 15, 1982

Vincente Minnelli

Date and Place of Birth	Date and Place of Death
February 28, 1903 Chicago, Illinois	July 25, 1986 812 North Crescent Drive Beverly Hills, California

Just a Matter of Time

B est known for his deft direction of grand and romantic Hollywood song-and-dance productions, Vincente Minnelli wrote in his autobiography entitled *I Remember It Well,* "I work to please myself. I'm still not sure if movies are an art form. And if they're not, then let them inscribe on my tombstone what they could about any craftsman who loves his job, 'Here lies Vincente Minnelli. He died of hard work.'"

Minnelli married the talented and volatile actress Judy Garland in 1946, shortly after she had completed her starring role in a movie being directed by Minnelli called *Meet Me in St. Louis.* Five years later, in 1951, Garland filed for divorce, claiming in part that Minnelli "secluded himself and wouldn't explain why he would be away and leave me alone so much." During their marriage, they had one daughter, Liza. Referring to his former wife Judy, who had died in 1969, and his Academy Award–winning daughter, Liza, Minnelli wrote, "How many men can lay claim to being loved by the most extraordinary talents of not one, but two generations? And who loved, not always wisely, in return? But love is what life is all about. Love of wife, love of family, love of work."

Besides Liza and Judy, Vincente found the time to love his second and third wives, Georgette Magnani and Denise Gigante. Unfortunately, both of those marriages also ended in divorce. During his second marriage, Minnelli had a second daughter, named Christiane Nina. At the time of his death, Minnelli was married to his fourth wife, formerly Lee Anderson. As succinctly stated in his 1982 Will:

> I declare that I am married to LEE ANDERSON MINNELLI, formerly known as LEE ANDERSON, and that all references to "my wife" in this Codicil [*sic*] and hereafter, shall be to her. I have two (2) children, namely, LIZA MINNELLI GERO, and CHRISTIANE NINA MINNELLI MIRO. I have no deceased children.

In his Will, Minnelli refers to an "Antenuptial Agreement between myself and my wife, then LEE ANDERSON, dated March 6, 1980, which Agreement is incorporated herein by reference." Perhaps due to or in spite of that antenuptial agreement, Minnelli makes a $50,000 bequest to his wife, Lee. He also makes a $5,000 bequest to his second daughter Christiane Nina. Referring to the $5,000 bequest to his second daughter, the Will states, "The amount of this gift is with the recognition that my daughter, CHRISTIANE NINA MINNELLI MIRO, is financially well provided for already."

Despite the reference to one daughter's financial well-being, Minnelli gives "all my tangible property, including my household furnishings, jewelry, memorabilia, works of art and any automobiles to which I hold title" and his entire residuary estate to his other daughter, Liza, who was not exactly a pauper herself. In addition, Minnelli made the following devise to Liza:

> I give my real property situated in Los Angeles County, California, and commonly known as 812 North Crescent Drive, Beverly Hills, California, together with any

insurance on the property, to my daughter, LIZA MIN-
NELLI GERO, if she survives me....

In deference to his wife, Minnelli includes the following
"wish" in the article giving the real property outright to Liza:

...it is my wish that my wife, LEE ANDERSON MIN-
NELLI, be permitted to continue to occupy the house
on this real property, furnished substantially as it is at
my death, during her life time, without payment of costs
and maintenance of the home (excluding food, daily
supplies and the like). In the event my daughter, LIZA
MINNELLI GERO or her issue decide it is necessary to
sell or occupy this real property, then it is my wish that
a suitable apartment or other place of residence be provided on the same terms as above stated.

Liza was clearly being designated to "wear the pants" after
father was somewhere over the rainbow with her mother.
However, not taking any chances that his estate's disposition
would be contested, Minnelli's Will also included the basic
in terrorem clause.

In a codicil that he signed a year after his Will, Minnelli
increased the bequest to his wife from $50,000 to $100,000.

Despite his often climactic endings on the silver screen,
Minnelli wanted his own exit to be quiet and inconspicuous.
His Will simply states:

This will confirm my previously stated desire that upon
my death my remains be cremated, and that there be
no funeral services.

As one might have guessed, Minnelli appointed his daughter Liza as the sole executor of his Will. It is ironic that, like

Henry Fonda, Minnelli died shortly after completing a film starring his daughter, entitled *A Matter of Time*.

/S/ *Vincente Minnelli*

WILL DATED: March 25, 1982
CODICIL DATED: June 23, 1983
SIGNED AT: Beverly Hills, California

John Cassavetes

Date and Place of Birth	Date and Place of Death
December 9, 1929 New York, New York	February 3, 1989 Los Angeles, California

A Man Under the Influence

Like many of his films, the one-page, handwritten Will of director and actor John Cassavetes is an example of his truthful and direct style. Cassavetes's Will bluntly and simply states:

> I leave all and everything I own or will own to my beloved wife, Gena Rowlands Cassavetes.
> I leave nothing to any one else, whomsoever, they may be.
> I owe no one any debt or obligation, other than usual and ordinary bills.
> No one has done me a special service that I feel obligated to.
> I hereby appoint my wife, Gena Executor of this Will ...

Cassavetes had been married to Gena Rowlands for over thirty years. She had appeared in several of her husband's films and won an award at the 1980 Venice Film Festival for her role in the film *Gloria*.

Besides his wife, Cassavetes was survived by his three children—Nicholas, Alexandra, and Zoe. It is a good thing that Cassavetes's wife survived him because there were no provisions for the guardians of his children or a successor executor

if she had not. From this bare-bones Will, it is clear that
Cassavetes's calling was as a filmmaker, not as a Will drafter.

/S/ *John Cassavetes*

WILL DATED: June 3, 1988
Will signed at 7917 Woodrow Wilson Drive
Los Angeles, California

THE ARTISTS

Art Is Long, Life Is Short

The Artist	Date of Death
Mark Rothko Art "Appreciation"	February 25, 1970
Norman Rockwell No More Rock in Stock	November 8, 1978
Georgia O'Keeffe Above New York and Below New Mexico	March 6, 1986
Andy Warhol "Death Means a Lot of Money, Honey"	February 22, 1987
Louise Nevelson Mother Knows Best	April 17, 1988
Robert Mapplethorpe Lights Out	March 9, 1989

Mark Rothko

Date and Place of Birth

September 25, 1903
Dvinsk, Russia

Date and Place of Death

February 25, 1970
157 East 69th Street
New York, New York

Art "Appreciation"

The painter whose life and death changed the course of art and artists' estates was named Marcus Rothkovich at his birth in the Latvian region of Russia, but the world knew him simply as "Rothko." It was during the 1940s and 1950s that Rothko became a leader of a loosely knit group of artists labeled "abstract expressionists" (a label he disdained) in New York.

Rothko's large-scale paintings dating from the late 1940s until his suicide in 1970 were outpourings of human emotions ranging from tragedy to ecstasy. Rothko's earliest abstract works were greeted with skepticism by many in the postwar art world. For the painter and his much younger second wife (he had been married first to Edith Sacher in the early 1930s and divorced from her in the 1940s), Mary Alice ("Mell") Beistle, those were years of struggle and sacrifice. But in the early 1950s, a new artistic consciousness arose among some in the art world who began to take notice of an emerging cadre of "abstract expressionists."

Increasingly critically acclaimed, in 1958 Rothko was commissioned by the wealthy Bronfman family of the Seagram company to paint a series of murals to hang in modern architecture's monolith on New York's Park Avenue bearing the family name. The Seagram Building was being designed by

Mies van der Rohe and Philip Johnson. The Rothko paintings were to hang in the The Four Seasons restaurant, which, since its opening, has for over one hundred seasons catered to the tastes of the most wealthy and powerful people in New York. For reasons that are not fully documented, Rothko himself allegedly canceled the prestigious Seagram commission, withdrew the completed paintings, and reportedly returned $14,000 that he had already received of the total commission of $35,000.

As Rothko's Will makes evident, these Four Seasons paintings had special significance for Rothko. The second article of his Will bequeaths to "the Tate Gallery, London, England, five (5) paintings of their choice of those paintings which were created by me for the Seagram Building, New York in 1959." In this one respect, the artist's wishes were honored, as these paintings, and others by Rothko, can be found today in special rooms devoted to Rothko's work in London's Tate Gallery.

With failing health leading to increased alcoholism and depression, Rothko's twenty-five-year marriage to Mell showed strain, and the two were separated in the fall of 1968. It was around that time that Rothko signed his last Will, dated September 13, 1968.

In that last Will, Rothko gives Mell the 118 East 95th Street town house he owned, "together with all of the contents thereof" (including all the paintings therein, as subsequently determined in a "construction proceeding" brought in the New York Surrogate's Court) and a $250,000 bequest. The Will provided further that if his wife did not survive him, then that property was to be equally divided between his two children, Kate and Christopher. The balance of his estate, including hundreds of paintings worth millions of dollars, was left to the not-yet-formed "MARK ROTHKO FOUNDA-TION," whose charitable purposes were not defined in his Will. In the Will, the foundation was vaguely described as "a non-profit organization, incorporated under the laws of the State of New York." The value of Rothko's estate was reportedly $30 million when he died, and $50 million by the time the precedent-setting case of *Matter of Rothko* had concluded.

Rothko's two-page Will was prepared by his longtime accountant, Bernard J. Reis. Reis and two other friends of Rothko's, painter Theodoros Stamos and anthropologist/professor Morton Levine, were named as the executors of Rothko's Will.

To control the undefined multimillion-dollar foundation, the Will states: "The Directors of the Foundation are to be: William Rubin [Museum of Modern Art curator], ROBERT GOLDWATER [Rothko's designated biographer], BERNARD J. REIS, THEODOROS STAMOS and MORTON LEVINE." It is ironic that Reis's secretary, who typed the Will, left William Rubin's name in lowercase letters and put the other names in all capital letters because Rubin would be dropped as a director of the foundation before Rothko's death.

The vibrations caused by *Matter of Rothko* have had a major impact upon the art world. The problems arose from a poorly conceived and drafted Will. Besides the divided loyalties and conflicts of interest rife within the Rothko estate, the purpose of the "MARK ROTHKO FOUNDATION" was nowhere defined. The executors ostensibly wanted to give grants to aging artists in need (which would also allow them to liquidate the estate's assets, thereby "earning" substantial commissions for themselves). On the other side was daughter Kate Rothko, who claimed that her father always wanted his paintings kept in groups and hung in the proper environments. The Will itself demonstrates Rothko's concern with the issue of keeping certain paintings together, as shown by the initial bequest of five paintings to the Tate Gallery.

When Surrogate Millard L. Midonick handed down his opinion in 1977, Kate Rothko, her brother, Christopher, and the art-loving public won hands down. The Surrogate decreed that all three executors were to be removed and replaced by Kate Rothko as the sole administrator of the estate. The contracts with the Marlborough Gallery were voided in toto, and the three executors were assessed surcharges, fines, and damages amounting to over $9 million. All the Rothko artworks that had not been removed by the Marlborough Gallery were ordered returned to the estate. Half of those artworks were given equally to the two Rothko children (Mell Rothko died only six months after her husband's death), and the other half were given to the Mark Rothko Foundation to be distributed to art museums and other institutions as the newly constituted Foundation Board deemed appropriate. After protracted appeals, the New York Court of Appeals upheld Surrogate Midonick's decision in 1977, finally ending the litigation over the artist's estate seven years after his death.

Both Bernard Reis and Morton Levine have died. Artist Theodoros Stamos is still being shown by the Marlborough Gallery. Stamos reportedly spends most of his time painting on the Greek island of Lefkada. The foundation wound up the core of its activities in 1986, sixteen years after the death of the artist. The artworks were distributed to approximately thirty museums in the United States and abroad, with most of them going to the National Gallery of Art in Washington.

Rothko's daughter, Kate, is now a doctor, is married, and has two children. Christopher Rothko was graduated from Yale University and is pursuing an interest in music. Those who find themselves staring into the depths of Mark Rothko's magnificent paintings may briefly forget the disconcerting relationships between great art and money that often lie beneath the surface.

/S/ *Mark Rothko*

WILL DATED: September 13, 1968

Norman Rockwell

Date and Place of Birth

February 3, 1894
New York, New York

Date and Place of Death

November 8, 1978
Stockbridge, Massachusetts

No More Rock in Stock

One of the most popular American artists of his times, Norman Rockwell was best known for his memorable cover illustrations of *The Saturday Evening Post*. The subject matter was invariably wholesome and usually in a country setting, but later in his career, Rockwell created pictures addressing pressing social issues. He may have had his artistic detractors for being an "illustrator" and not an artist, but there can be no doubt that Norman Rockwell's art has touched the hearts of millions of people.

Rockwell was married three times. His first marriage, to Irene O'Connor, lasted from 1916 until ending in divorce in 1928. Two years later, Rockwell married a California teacher named Mary Rhodes Barstow. Together, Norman and Mary had three sons—Jarvis, Thomas, and Peter. The Rockwells first lived in Vermont, but later settled into a carriage house with a studio in Stockbridge, Massachusetts. Mary Rockwell died in 1959. In 1961, Rockwell married his third and final wife, Mary L. Punderson.

In his Will Rockwell leaves all of his tangible property and his residential property, excluding his studio and the contents thereof, to his wife, Mary. For the studio of the great draftsman and painter, the Will provides in "CLAUSE FIRST":

> I give, devise and bequeath to the NORMAN ROCKWELL
> ART COLLECTION TRUST...the building which I have

used as my studio together with the contents thereof
at the time of my death, including but not limited to
any works of art done by me or others...

This provision was supplemented by a second codicil to Rockwell's Will which he signed shakily a few months before his
death, which provides:

I hereby add the following sentence to CLAUSE FIRST:
Notwithstanding the foregoing, this bequest is conditioned upon the payments by Old Corner House, Inc., a
charitable corporation located in said Stockbridge, of
all expenses of removing said studio from said real estate and regrading and relandscaping said real estate
so as to restore the same to an attractive and aesthet-
ically appealing condition following such removal, and
of any other costs in any way connected with or related
to the fulfillment of this bequest, and if such condition
is not satisfied, this bequest shall lapse...

Such a conditional bequest was a clever way to be sure that
the work would be done properly and that the cost would be
borne by the recipient of this artistic gold mine. Today, Rockwell's studio is not open to the public, but it will become a
part of the new Norman Rockwell Museum scheduled to be
opened in Stockbridge in 1993.

Under his Will Rockwell established a $500,000 trust for
the benefit of his wife. The balance of Rockwell's estate was
to be divided into equal shares for each of his three sons and
held in trust for them for their lives. Income could also be
paid to any widowed daughters-in-law until such time as she
might remarry, and the remainder was left for his grandchildren. Rockwell took a trustworthy approach when dividing
his estate.

In his Will Rockwell named his wife, Mary L. Punderson
Rockwell, and one of his three sons, Thomas Rhodes Rockwell,

as his executors. However, in a later codicil to that Will Rockwell added the Berkshire Bank and Trust Company as a co-executor with his wife and son.

As trustees, Rockwell named his wife, son Thomas, and the Berkshire Bank. If Thomas could not act, then Rockwell designated his son Peter to act, or if he could not act, he named his son Jarvis. However, in the first codicil to his Will Rockwell changed the successor executor designation to provide that if either his wife or son could not act, that no successor executor needed to be added. Regarding his trustees, Rockwell's codicil continued:

> In the event no one of my said three sons shall be able or willing to serve or to continue to serve, I direct that the oldest adult grandchild of mine who is willing and able to serve as Trustee hereunder...shall serve as a successor Trustee together with said bank...

Apparently, Rockwell believed that one of the trustees of his wife's or sons' trusts should always be a family member, in addition to the bank.

The great sensitivity to family relationships depicted in Norman Rockwell's art shows itself in the artist's own Will. It is often said that art imitates life, but in Norman Rockwell's case, life also imitated art.

/S/ *Norman Rockwell*

WILL DATED: December 9, 1976
1ST CODICIL: June 17, 1977
2ND CODICIL: May 29, 1978

Georgia O'Keeffe

Date and Place of Birth	Date and Place of Death
November 15, 1887 Sun Prairie, Wisconsin	March 6, 1986 St. Vincent's Hospital Santa Fe, New Mexico

Above New York and Below New Mexico

Georgia O'Keeffe was one of the unique artistic forces of the twentieth century. In 1916 she had a one-woman exhibition of her paintings at famed photographer Alfred Stieglitz's legendary "291" Fifth Avenue gallery in New York. That show established O'Keeffe as an important emerging artist; she continued to delight critics until her death seventy years later at the age of ninety-eight.

O'Keeffe's relationship with Stieglitz was more than merely professional. They were married in 1924 and collaborated personally and professionally until Stieglitz's death twenty-one years later. After Stieglitz's death, O'Keeffe left the urban sprawl of New York and went to live in the starkly contrasting desert of New Mexico. With the change of landscape, O'Keeffe's art continued to express a deeply individualistic spirit.

After O'Keeffe had settled in her studio in an Abiquiu, New Mexico, ranch a new man appeared in her life. A young potter named "Juan" (not Don) Hamilton appeared at O'Keeffe's door one day looking for work and never left. Hamilton certainly won the trust and love of an opinionated and often brusque woman. He assisted O'Keeffe with the production of a book about her and a documentary film and attended to all the other things that a nonagenarian might want and need from a man in his thirties.

In her 1979 Will, made when she was ninety-one years old, O'Keeffe gives:

> all my right, title and interest to my ranch, consisting of a house and acreage located outside of Abiquiu, in the County of Rio Arriba and State of New Mexico, which was formerly part of the "Ghost Ranch"...together with the furnishings therein...to my friend, JOHN BRUCE HAMILTON, or if he does not survive me, to THE UNITED PRESBYTERIAN CHURCH IN THE UNITED STATES OF AMERICA, located at 475 Riverside Drive, New York, New York, for its general purposes.

In addition, Mr. Hamilton was allowed to select any six of O'Keeffe's paintings on canvas and any fifteen works from among O'Keeffe's drawings, watercolors, or pastels not otherwise disposed of in the Will.

O'Keeffe specifically bequeathed certain paintings to each of eight museums expressly named in her Will: The Art Institute of Chicago, Boston's Museum of Fine Arts, New York's Modern, Metropolitan, and Brooklyn museums, the Cleveland Museum of Art, the Philadelphia Museum of Art, and The National Gallery in Washington, D.C. In addition, The National Gallery of Art received "all photographs of me taken by my late husband, ALFRED STIEGLITZ, which are presently on loan to said institution." She gave all her "letters, personal correspondence and clippings to YALE UNIVERSITY." All the rest of "my writings and papers, together with all copyrights thereon and rights of publication thereto," she gave to "my friend, JOHN BRUCE HAMILTON."

As one might have expected, O'Keeffe appointed Mr. Hamilton as the sole executor of her Will. In a 1983 codicil, his fee for acting as executor is limited to a not-so-mere $200,000.

We need not be concerned about the plight of Mr. Hamilton because in a 1984 second codicil to her Will, O'Keeffe gives her entire residuary estate to "my friend, JOHN BRUCE HAMILTON." If Hamilton failed to survive her, O'Keeffe's estate would pass as *he* would appoint under his own Will. The changes made by this last codicil are even more incredible as that clause concludes, "In default of [John Bruce Hamilton's] effective exercise of this power of appointment, my residuary estate shall instead be distributed among the heirs of John Bruce Hamilton as if he had died intestate." The ninety-six-year-old's signature on that final codicil is very shaky. It is interesting to note that on the probate petition submitted with the Will and codicils, the "John Bruce Hamilton" mentioned repeatedly in the Will signed his name as "Juan Hamilton." Let's hope that at least O'Keeffe had the right man in mind.

That same codicil giving O'Keeffe's entire residuary estate to Hamilton also includes a one-dollar *in terrorem* clause just in case anyone was considering contesting the disposition of her estate. O'Keeffe was survived by a sister named Catherine Klernet. Sister Catherine lived in Portage, Wisconsin, and is not mentioned in sister Georgia's Will.

Finally, the Will makes no mention of O'Keeffe's burial, funeral, or cremation provisions. O'Keeffe's attorney said that she had been cremated and her ashes would be scattered in New Mexico, but he would not reveal where or when. "Ashes to ashes, dust to dust"; it seems fitting that the last remains of Georgia O'Keeffe should be spread on the desert lands that she had loved.

/S/ *Georgia O'Keeffe*

WILL DATED: August 22, 1979
1ST CODICIL DATED: November 2, 1983
2ND CODICIL DATED: August 8, 1984

Andy Warhol

Date and Place of Birth	Date and Place of Death
August 6, 1928 (?) Pittsburgh, Pennsylvania	February 22, 1987 New York Hospital New York, New York

"Death Means a Lot of Money, Honey"

The pop of Pop, Andy Warhol, died with a multifaceted estate estimated to be worth in excess of $75 million. Yet under his Will he bequeathed $750,000 (less than 1 percent of the total value) to only three people—his two brothers, John and Paul, and "my friend, FREDERICK HUGHES," the man who gave him life-saving mouth-to-mouth resuscitation after Warhol's near fatal shooting in 1968. Warhol also named Mr. Hughes as his sole executor. Many have said that after Warhol's death, Hughes actually exercised more power than Warhol ever did. Hughes quickly sold Warhol's non-Warhol art and collectibles, netting over $25 million for the estate, and later sold *Interview Magazine* for a reported sum of $14 million.

Even in Warhol's bequest to his two brothers, Warhol gave Hughes unusually broad discretion. The third article of the Will states:

> I give such portion of my residuary estate as my friend, FREDERICK HUGHES (or, if my said friend shall not survive me, my friend, VINCENT FREEMONT), shall validly appoint in equal shares, to such of my brothers, JOHN WARHOL [sic] and PAUL WARHOL [sic], as shall survive me, by the exercise of a power of appointment

over such portion of my residuary estate contained in
an instrument in writing duly signed and acknowledged
by my said friend and delivered to my Executor within
six (6) months after the issuance of Letters Testamentary to my Executor; provided, however, that such portion of my residuary estate shall not exceed the sum of
Five Hundred Thousand ($500,000) Dollars....

One has to wonder what kind of consideration was given
to allow one person the option to give Warhol's own two
brothers (whose names are misspelled in the Will) nothing
from his vast estate. As it turned out, each of Warhol's brothers
received the maximum possible bequest under the Will—
$250,000, the same as Fred Hughes himself. However, as
executor and director of the Foundation for Visual Arts (discussed below), Hughes also stood to make millions of dollars
in commissions.

With Warhol's gargantuan collection of cookie jars, bronzes,
Fiesta ware, cigar-store Indians, watches, funeral urns, toys,
jewelry, furniture, and other collectibles, seminal modern-art
collection, and an estate holding eight separate parcels of real
estate in New York, Montauk, and Colorado, one wonders
whether Warhol ever considered the possibilities of establishing the Pop Art Museum or doing something more
thoughtful with his estate. Instead, Warhol left the vast portion of his estate to a nebulous foundation, "THE FOUN-
DATION FOR VISUAL ARTS," which had not even been
incorporated at the time of Warhol's death.

One of three sons of immigrant parents from Czechoslo-
vakia, Andrew Warhola got a degree in pictorial design from
Carnegie Institute of Technology (now Carnegie-Mellon University) and headed for New York in 1950. He dropped the
a in Warhola and became a successful women's shoe (among
other items) illustrator. In 1962, Warhol hit his mark and
began to mirror America's consumer and voyeuristic society
back at itself by exhibiting larger-than-life icons such as the

Campbell's soup can, a Brillo box, or the late Marilyn Monroe.

Later, a darker side emerged in Warhol's art as he depicted images of death and disasters, including his arresting sequential images of the assassination of President Kennedy, an empty and waiting electric chair, or the scene of a fatal car crash. It has been observed that lurking beneath almost all of Warhol's paintings is the color black.

An assassination attempt by a disgruntled former Factory worker in 1968 turned Warhol even more inward. Themes of death played an important part throughout Warhol's entire artistic oeuvre as his late works include a series of skull paintings strangely reminiscent of the *memento mori* (or reminders of death) in Renaissance paintings.

In the late 1970s, Warhol emerged from his artistic shell and became a court painter for the rich and famous. At a minimum of $25,000 per portrait, Warhol was able to generate enough cash to support his many infamous film projects and a periodical that served to institutionalize Pop Culture—*Interview Magazine*.

Warhol was notoriously afraid of going to the doctor and hospitals. (He also attended church religiously.) In light of Warhol's concerns about medical care, it is ironic that his death from a heart attack, after his condition was termed "stable" following an elective gall bladder operation, occurred at five-thirty A.M. when Warhol was left alone in his room in one of New York's best hospitals.

Warhol's death came at a time in his life when he had been rejuvenated by the friendships and collaborations with a younger generation of artists, particularly Jean-Michel Basquiat. Basquiat's own drug-overdose death a year and a half later in the Great Jones Street studio, which he had rented from Warhol and then from Warhol's estate, was said to be indirectly related to Warhol's death. In artists such as Basquiat, Keith Haring, Kenny Scharf, and Ronnie Cutrone, Warhol saw a new breed of 1980s-style Pop artists with graffiti-art roots and whose friendships meant much to Warhol. It is noteworthy that Cutrone, who worked as one of Warhol's assistants, was also one of the witnesses to his Will when it was signed in 1982, at 860 Broadway, one of the Factory sites. Evidently, Warhol did not want to go to his fancy Park Avenue lawyers' offices to sign a Will, so an associate from that prestigious law firm was apparently hastily dispatched* to supervise the Will's execution.

In light of the radical and drastic changes wrought on Warhol's estate after his death, one wonders whether the proper attention was directed toward estate planning for the unusual Andy Warhol. Shortly before he died, Warhol could not have been more correct when he prophetically stated in a videotape, "Death means a lot of money, honey."

/S/ Andy Warhol

*Will dated March 11, 1982. (The Will had apparently first been prepared in 1981, but that year was crossed out in five places on the Will and witnesses' affidavit and the year 1982 was inserted.)

Louise Nevelson

Date and Place of Birth

September 23, 1899
Kiev, Russia

Date and Place of Death

April 17, 1988
29 Spring Street
New York, New York

Mother Knows Best

One of the leading sculptors of the twentieth century, Louise Nevelson created monumental works that were often moody and mysterious. After a major retrospective of her works at the Museum of Modern Art in 1967, Nevelson's sculptures were quite valuable by the time she died. Her estate was reportedly worth almost $100 million. Not bad for the daughter of Russian immigrants—named Isaac and Minna Berliawsky—who had first settled at the age of five in the unlikely town of Rockland, Maine.

In her autobiography, called *Dawns and Dusks*, Nevelson says that she had always wanted to be an artist. About Rockland, Maine, Nevelson said, "I never made friends because I didn't intend to stay in Rockland, and I didn't want anything to tie me down." In 1920 she married Charles Nevelson and they moved to New York City, which would be Nevelson's home until the day she died. In 1922, the Nevelsons' only child, named Myron, was born. Eight years later, the marriage was disintegrating, and young Myron was reportedly tossed back and forth from father to mother and back to father again. Eventually, son Myron, who used the name Mike, left town on a merchant ship during World War II and was married three times by the time of his mother's death.

Nevelson's 1974 Will is about as simple and straightforward

as they come. She leaves her entire estate to "my son, Mike Nevelson"; if Mike did not survive her, then to Mike's "issue surviving me in equal shares per stirpes" (which is a contradiction in legal terms). The property was to be held in trust for any of her issue who might inherit property and be under the age of twenty-one. It is noteworthy that Nevelson herself had gained her own independence around the age of twenty-one.

Son Mike was the only person individually named in his mother's Will, other than his mother. Mike is named as the sole executor of the Will. The Will did include the following thirty-day survivorship provision:

> In the event that any beneficiary hereunder shall survive me, but shall die within thirty (30) days after the date of my death, then all the provisions of this Will shall take effect in like manner as if said beneficiary had predeceased me.

Presumably, Mike looked both ways when crossing the street for at least thirty days after his mother's death. He met the thirty-day survivorship requirement and inherited his mother's entire estate. Mike Nevelson also met Diana Mackowan.

Reportedly for the last twenty-five years of her life, Nevelson had been attended to and assisted by a woman named Diana Mackowan. Mackowan claimed that she had been given many of Nevelson's sculptures over the years. Furthermore, Mackowan claimed that she was entitled to compensation amounting to $325,000 for her many years of service. Son and executor Mike rejected her claim for any compensation, attempted to evict her from the building that she had occupied for many years, and withheld the sculptures allegedly belonging to Miss Mackowan. The feud between the two has been unusually vitriolic and has divided Nevelson's art-world friends.

The battle over the estate is still being fought, but the question must be asked why Nevelson never updated her rather skimpy 1974 Will to make provision for her friend Diana Mackowan, if that is what she wanted to do. From Mike Nevelson's perspective, mother knew best.

/S/ *Louise Nevelson*

WILL DATED: May 3, 1974

Robert Mapplethorpe

Date and Place of Birth

November 4, 1946
Floral Park, New York

Date and Place of Death

March 9, 1989
New England Deaconess
  Hospital
Boston, Massachusetts

Lights Out

According to personal accounts, handsome photographer Robert Mapplethorpe was as much a participant as a voyeur hiding behind his camera. Tragically, Mapplethorpe died from complications of acquired immune deficiency syndrome (AIDS). One of the most important influences in Mapplethorpe's life had been his companion, major art collector, and patron, Sam Wagstaff. Before he died of AIDS himself in 1987, Wagstaff had assembled one of the greatest photography collections ever, reportedly valued at $20 million, which he eventually sold to the Getty Museum. Wagstaff named his younger friend Robert Mapplethorpe as the primary beneficiary and executor of his estate. In that regard, Mapplethorpe's own Will provides:

> In the event that at the time of my death the administration of the Estate of Samuel J. Wagstaff, Jr., in which I have a substantial interest, has not been completed, I direct my executor to apply for letters of administration C.T.A. with respect to said estate and to complete the administration of said estate.

("C.T.A." describes the administration of an estate by a person not named in the Will, but who has been appointed to act *cum testamento annexo,* Latin for "with the Will annexed.")

Mapplethorpe is very generous to many friends named in his Will. He makes bequests ranging from $100,000 to $2,500 to almost twenty different people. One of the recipients of a $100,000 bequest is Mapplethorpe's former girlfriend, rock star Patti Smith. Mapplethorpe also establishes a $230,000 trust fund for the benefit of his friend Jack Walls. One other friend is the legatee of a "Fang wood reliquary figure from Gabon."

Mapplethorpe was survived by his father, mother, two brothers, and two sisters. His parents are not mentioned in his Will. One of his sisters gets a $10,000 bequest. To his brother Edward, who aided him during his last illness, Mapplethorpe made the following bequest:

> I give the sum of $100,000 and such of my photographic equipment as he shall select to my brother, EDWARD MAPPLETHORPE, if he survives me.

Brother Ed survived and is using some of his late brother's photographic equipment today and operating under the nom de camera of Edward Maxey (which was mother Mapplethorpe's maiden name).

The bulk of Mapplethorpe's estate was left to The Robert Mapplethorpe Foundation, Inc., which he had established before he died. That foundation was established for the purposes of medical research, especially AIDS research, and for the visual arts, especially photography. Photography and AIDS—the two things that Mapplethorpe had lived for and died of respectively.

As his executor, Mapplethorpe appoints his attorney and trusted adviser, Michael Ward Stout. It appears that Stout had advised his client of the significant executor's commissions and fees he would earn as an executor of an estate of such size and property. But Mapplethorpe did not seem to mind, as in his Will he states:

> I am presently serving as executor of a substantial es-
> tate [Sam Wagstaff's] and am fully familiar with the
> duties of an executor and the compensation to which
> an executor is entitled to receive under the law of New
> York. I anticipate that the administration of my estate
> will be very time consuming and will require consid-
> erable skill and I direct that my executor and my trustee
> shall receive full statutory commissions.

Later, it gets thicker, as the Will states:

> I have appointed as fiduciaries persons with whom I
> presently have business associations. Michael Ward
> Stout, my designated executor and trustee, has served
> me as my attorney for more than five years, under dif-
> ficult circumstances, and has served with great dis-
> tinction. He is far more familiar than any other
> individual with my business activities and with my
> wishes with respect to the disposition of works of art
> which I have created as well as with respect to works
> created by others which I have collected. He is a spe-
> cialist in the law of intellectual and artistic properties
> as well as a close and trusted personal friend.

With language such as that, it is not surprising that mom and
pop Mapplethorpe chose not to contest the Will. They would
have been their wealthy son's only heirs if he had not had a
Will.

Two days before he died a slow and painful death from
AIDS in a Boston hospital, Mapplethorpe made additional
bequests of either $2,500 or $5,000 to three other people. His
attorney wisely chose to make this change by a codicil to the
Will rather than by preparing a new Will with Mapplethorpe
already so close to death. In that way, the Will itself would
be less subject to attack as that of a seriously debilitated man;
only the last codicil would be at risk. That last codicil was

admitted to probate and those three individuals received their bequests.

Mapplethorpe's signature on the codicil is a jagged example of the signature of the photographer. In life, he had lived on the edge, and he fell over the edge at the age of forty-two, after leaving a legacy of controversy and photography that history and society would never forget.

/S/ *Robert Mapplethorpe*

WILL DATED: June 23, 1988
CODICIL DATED: March 7, 1989

ONE OF A KIND

The One

Albert Einstein
Personal Theories of Relativity

Date of Death

April 19, 1955

Albert Einstein

Date and Place of Birth	Date and Place of Death
March 14, 1879 Württemberg, Germany	April 19, 1955 Princeton Hospital Princeton, New Jersey

Personal Theories of Relativity

When he died in his sleep at the age of seventy-six, brilliant scientist, physicist, and pacifist Albert Einstein left a legacy of revolutionary scientific concepts that changed the world's view of itself.

For all his great achievements, Einstein had an inauspicious start, with his often-cited poor grades in school and then as an unknown clerk in a Swiss patent office. In 1901, Einstein married a Swiss student named Mileva Marec. Together, they had two sons—Albert Einstein, Jr., and Eduard Einstein. Subsequently, that marriage ended in divorce. In 1919, Einstein married his second cousin, Elsa Einstein, a widow with two daughters. She remained married to Einstein until her death in 1936 in Princeton, New Jersey. Einstein never again married before his own death almost twenty years later. However, Einstein did have a "secretary-housekeeper" named Helena Dukas for many years. Einstein's Will, which he signed in 1950, makes it quite clear that Helena Dukas was his top priority above and beyond Einstein's own relatives. Apparently, Einstein maintained certain personal theories of relativity.

Under his Will, Einstein gives to "my secretary, Helena Dukas... all of my personal clothing and personal effects, except my violin..." Einstein also established a trust to hold "all of my manuscripts, copyrights, publication rights, royalties and royalty agreements, and all other literary property and rights, of any and every kind or nature whatsoever." The income from that trust was to be paid to secretary Helena Dukas and then upon her death to stepdaughter Margot Einstein. Upon the death of both Margot and Helena, the property was to be delivered to the Hebrew University in Israel. In this article creating this trust for his manuscripts, Einstein states:

> In the interpretation of this provision of my will, it is to be borne in mind that my primary object is to make further provision for the care, comfort and welfare of my said secretary, HELENA DUKAS, during her lifetime; my secondary object is to make such further provision for the care, comfort and welfare of my said step-daughter, MARGOT EINSTEIN, during her lifetime; and my final object is that any such property which may then remain (whether it consist of original manuscripts, or literary rights or property still owned by my estate, or the proceeds from the disposition of any such property or rights) shall to the extent that the same shall not have been distributed or paid over to my said secretary and my said step-daughter, pass to HEBREW UNIVERSITY and become its property absolutely, to be thereafter retained or disposed of by it as it may deem to be in its best interests...

To his stepdaughter Margot Einstein, who lived in Einstein's Princeton home with Albert and Miss Dukas, Einstein bequeathed "all of my furniture and household goods, chattels and effects, of every kind or nature." The parameters of "every kind or nature" to the mind of Albert Einstein must be left open to speculation.

Einstein made the following cash bequests under his Will: $20,000 each to stepdaughter Margot and secretary Helena,

$15,000 to son Eduard, $10,000 to son Albert Einstein, Jr., or if he predeceased Einstein, to Einstein's favorite grandchild, Bernhard Caesar Einstein. A $10,000 trust was also established for the benefit of Albert's sister, Marie Winteler.

Einstein's violin was bequeathed to his grandson, Bernhard Caesar Einstein, with the provision that "if he shall not be of legal age, then I authorize and empower my Executors to deliver the same to his father, my son Albert Einstein, Jr., in his behalf, to be turned over to my said grandson when he shall attain majority." It seems to have been quite important to Einstein that his grandson be able to fiddle around with his beloved violin.

Einstein gave the remaining portion of his estate to his stepdaughter Margot, or if she did not survive him, to his son Albert Einstein, Jr. The Will provides that "without limitation of the absolute nature of the bequest of my residuary estate," if his sister, Marie Winteler, survived him and the $10,000 trust fund established for her was exhausted, then he requested that his said son or stepdaughter make other or further provisions "for the care, comfort and welfare of my said sister, as long as she shall live."

Einstein's Will does not contain any provisions regarding his funeral or burial. It was reported that shortly after his death Einstein's body was cremated—but not before his vital organs, including his brain, were removed from his body for the purpose of scientific study. Einstein's brain was certainly a worthy specimen.

/S/ *Albert Einstein*

WILL DATED: March 18, 1950

THE SUPER RICH

You Can't Take It With You

The Super Rich	Date of Death
John Jacob Astor IV Chivalry Is Dead	April 15, 1912
J. Pierpont Morgan No Guarantees	March 31, 1913
Howard Hughes Summa, but Not Loud	April 5, 1976
J. Paul Getty Why Not to Marry a Billionaire	June 6, 1976
Conrad Hilton No More Room Service	January 3, 1979

Nelson A. Rockefeller   January 26, 1979
Happy in Camp Rockefeller

Malcolm Forbes   February 24, 1990
He Went Thataway . . .

John Jacob Astor IV

Date and Place of Birth	Date and Place of Death
July 13, 1864 Ferncliff Rhinebeck-on-the-Hudson, New York	April 15, 1912 *Titanic* Atlantic Ocean

Chivalry Is Dead

One of America's richest men in the early 1900s, with a fortune reportedly close to $200 million, Colonel John Jacob Astor IV owned more hotels and high-rise buildings than any other New Yorker. It is ironic that Astor, who was such a devotee of ships, died on the maiden voyage of the newest, grandest ocean liner of them all—the "unsinkable" *Titanic*. Reportedly, as the *Titanic* was sinking, Astor chivalrously made sure that all the women and children were put in the lifeboats before himself. As his pregnant wife left the sinking ship, Astor reportedly coolly lit a cigarette and said to his wife, "Good-bye, dearie. I'll see you later." He never did; his chivalry led to his demise.

In his Will, Astor makes the following special provisions for an annual yacht trophy fund:

> I DIRECT that the Executors of this my will...in each year until my son William Vincent Astor shall attain the age of twenty-one years or sooner die, pay to the NEW YORK YACHT CLUB the sum of FIFTEEN HUNDRED DOLLARS, to be used and applied by the said Club for the purchase of two silver cups as prizes, one of such cups to cost One thousand dollars, to be sailed

and competed for by the sloop yachts of the New York
Yacht Club; and I DIRECT that such prizes shall be
competed for at Newport, Rhode Island, on the cruise
of said Yacht Club during the month of August in each
year....

Unfortunately, the Big A did not make the 1912 yacht race.

Born to a patrician family, Astor attended St. Paul's School
in Concord, New Hampshire, and then attended Harvard
College. He made a $30,000 bequest to St. Paul's, but Harvard was not mentioned in his Will.

In 1894, Astor married Miss Ava L. Willing, who was *very*
willing. They had two children: William Vincent Astor, who
was in his late teens when his father died, and a daughter,
Alice, who was then ten. Apparently, the marriage was
stormy; they were divorced in November of 1909. The divorce
decree provided that father took son William and mother took
daughter Alice. Ava reportedly received $50,000 a year as
alimony and support payments.

In 1911, the forty-seven-year-old Astor was married to
eighteen-year-old Miss Madeleine Talmage Force in Newport, Rhode Island. Astor had found a new port in which to
dock. In his Will, which he signed one week after his marriage,
Astor bequeaths his residuary estate to his beloved son Vincent with the express intention of keeping certain assets
in the Astors' place. William Vincent gets all the land in
Rhinebeck, New York, and "all my jewelry, wearing apparel,
personal effects, and all my yachts and boats." There go those
boats again.

For his wife of one week, Astor provides:

THIRD: I GIVE AND DEVISE the plot of land situated
at the northeasterly corner of the Fifth Avenue and
Sixty-fifth Street, in the Borough of Manhattan, City of
New York... with the dwellings and stable thereon, together with the printed books, paintings, pictures, en-

gravings, marbles, bronzes, statuary and objects of art,
plate and silver plated ware, linen, china, glass, household furniture and effects, useful and ornamental, contained therein at the time of my death and not
hereinbefore otherwise disposed of, unto my wife,
MADELEINE TALMAGE FORCE ASTOR, to have and to
hold the same unto her for so long during her natural
life as she shall remain my widow, and upon her death
or re-marriage, whichever shall first happen, I GIVE,
DEVISE AND BEQUEATH all of the property in this article mentioned unto my son WILLIAM VINCENT AS-
TOR...

It should be noted that the Will provides that Madeleine's
life interest in the house and stables is revoked if Madeleine
remarries. Madeleine did eventually give it up for another
man a few years later. Next, the Will refers to "certain antenuptial settlements" that, even then, were de rigueur for
someone of Astor's background and marital history.

FOURTH: Having by certain ante-nuptial settlements
made certain provisions for the benefit of my wife, MA-
DELEINE TALMAGE FORCE ASTOR, I do make the following further provision for her:
     I GIVE, DEVISE AND BEQUEATH to the Executors
of this my will the sum of FIVE MILLION DOLLARS...
to be had and holden by them and their successors in
the trust as trustees, IN TRUST....
FIFTH: I GIVE AND BEQUEATH unto my said wife, MA-
DELEINE TALMAGE FORCE ASTOR, the sum of ONE
HUNDRED THOUSAND DOLLARS, payable immediately
upon my death, all horses and other live-stock and all
carriages and harness and stable furniture, and all automobiles, and all provisions and supplies which shall
belong to me...

One has to wonder what she used all the horses and other livestock for after J.J.A. was with the fishes.

Astor also remembers various friends, relatives, and employees with "token" bequests ranging from $10,000 to $30,000.

In the end it seems as though young William takes the grand prize, inheriting most of Astor's place. "ALL THE REST, RESIDUE AND REMAINDER of my property and estate, real and personal, of whatsoever kind and wheresoever situated... I GIVE, DEVISE AND BEQUEATH absolutely and in fee simple, unto my son WILLIAM VINCENT ASTOR." However, after the date of the Will's execution, John Jacob Astor V was in the making and was born in August 1912, about four months after his father's death.

Astor names his brother-in-law James Roosevelt, friends Douglas Robinson and Nicholas Biddle, and also his son William Vincent Astor, upon his attaining the age of twenty-one years, to be his executors and trustees. After naming them, the Will states "I GIVE to each of them who shall qualify and act as such Executor the sum of THIRTY-FIVE THOUSAND DOLLARS in lieu of commissions upon the capital of my estate." It is interesting to note that Mr. Moneybags, John Jacob Astor IV, chose to limit the commissions that each of his executors would have earned executing his multiasseted estate. Perhaps Astor placed a value on the honor of their serving on his behalf.

When Astor's body was finally recovered from the Atlantic ten days after the *Titanic* went down for the count, Astor reportedly had about $2,500 in cash in his pockets. Perhaps it was the weight of the great Astor fortune and holdings that in part brought the *Titanic* down.

/S/ *John Jacob Astor*

WILL DATED: September 18, 1911

J. Pierpont Morgan

Date and Place of Birth	Date and Place of Death
April 17, 1837 26 Asylum Street Hartford, Connecticut	March 31, 1913 The Grand Hotel Rome, Italy

No Guarantees

*W*hen the Will of the monarch of Wall Street and one of the greatest financiers of his era, John Pierpont Morgan, was made public, people were surprised to see that the first article reflected a deeply religious man:

> I commit my soul into the hands of my Saviour, in full confidence that having redeemed it and washed it in His most precious blood He will present it faultless before the throne of my Heavenly Father; and I entreat my children to maintain and defend, at all hazard, and at any cost of personal sacrifice, the blessed doctrine of the complete atonement for sin through the blood of Jesus Christ, once offered, and through that alone.

Despite his great fortunes and successes, Morgan did not apparently necessarily believe that the success of one life could guarantee success in the next life. Hence, his commitment into the hands of his Saviour, in full confidence that . . . his soul would be presented "faultless." For J. P.'s sake, let's hope so.

Next, the Will states Morgan's wishes regarding his burial, which reflected his close feelings for his family, particularly his father, Junius Spencer Morgan:

231

It is my desire to be buried in the family burial place prepared by my father in Cedar Hill Cemetery, at Hartford, Connecticut, and I HEREBY DIRECT that my body be there interred on the west of the monument and opposite the place where my father's remains are interred.

I wish that in all arrangements for my funeral the same general course be followed that was adopted in the case of my father, except that the service shall be held at St. George's Church in the City of New York, with the Bishops of New York, Connecticut and Massachusetts, and the Rector of St. George's officiating.

Morgan's wishes regarding his burial were respected by his family. Newspaper reports of his funeral state that after the service, held at St. George's Protestant Episcopal Church, a special train took Morgan's body from Grand Central Terminal in New York to Hartford, Connecticut, where the interment took place.

Morgan's Will, which was signed in January of the year he died, made the following provisions for Morgan's "beloved wife FRANCES," whom he had married in the same St. George's Church in 1865:

...I MAKE THE FOLLOWING GIFTS AND PROVISIONS to and for the benefit of my beloved wife FRANCES LOUISA TRACY MORGAN.

Section 1. I GIVE AND BEQUEATH unto my EXECUTORS and TRUSTEES the sum of ONE MILLION DOLLARS, IN TRUST...

Section 2. After my death my said wife will receive the income which will be produced by a certain trust fund now held by me as trustee under a deed of trust dated July 1st, 1867, made to me by my father Junius Spencer Morgan, which fund has been very largely increased during my lifetime.

Section 3. I GIVE, DEVISE AND BEQUEATH to my said wife for her own use during the term of her natural life, without impeachment of waste, my country place called "Cragston", in the Town of Highlands, in the County of Orange, in the State of New York...

AND I GIVE AND BEQUEATH unto my said wife absolutely for her own use all furniture, clothing, pictures (except family portraits) works of art, silver, plate, ornaments, bric-a-brac, household goods, or supplies, books, linen, china, glass, horses, carriages, automobiles, harness and stable furniture or equipment, and all implements, plants and tools, and all live stock, which may be in or upon my said country place at the time of my death or shall then be customarily used by me in connection therewith.

Section 4. I ALSO GIVE, DEVISE AND BEQUEATH to my said wife for her own use during the term of her natural life, without impeachment of waste, the lot of land in the Borough of Manhattan, City of New York, situated on the northeast corner of Madison Avenue and Thirty-sixth Street...together with all furniture, clothing, pictures (except family portraits) ...(except wines)...

After forty-eight years of marriage, Mrs. Morgan might have felt too old to enjoy it all herself. During the first ten years of their marriage the Morgans had four children: Louisa, who later married Herbert Satterlee and was by her father's bed when he died; John Pierpont Morgan, Jr., who stepped into his father's shoes as head of the family business in 1913; Juliet Pierpont, who later married William P. Hamilton; and Anne Tracy, who never married.

For his children, Morgan makes the following gifts and obviously has the idea that women should receive property in trust rather than outright:

Section 1. I GIVE AND BEQUEATH unto my son JOHN PIERPONT MORGAN, Junior, if he shall survive me, the sum of THREE MILLIONS OF DOLLARS....

Section 3. If my daughter LOUISA, wife of Herbert Livingston Satterlee, shall survive me, but not otherwise, I GIVE AND BEQUEATH unto my said executors and trustees the sum of THREE MILLIONS OF DOLLARS, IN TRUST....

Section 5. If my daughter, ANNE TRACY MORGAN, shall survive me, but not otherwise, I GIVE AND BEQUEATH unto my said executors and trustees the sum of THREE MILLIONS OF DOLLARS IN TRUST....

Section 8. I GIVE AND BEQUEATH unto my son-in-law WILLIAM PIERSON HAMILTON the sum of ONE MILLION DOLLARS.

There is also a provision for a million-dollar trust for the widow of his son, John, should he have predeceased his father.

Next, Morgan makes the following bequest of his prized wine collection to his son with the expectation that he would share the wine with sons-in-law and friends. Perhaps Morgan believed that his daughters should not be wine drinkers, but J. P. clearly wanted to keep the intoxicants in the Morgan family.

I GIVE AND BEQUEATH all my wines unto my said son JOHN PIERPONT MORGAN, Junior, or if he shall not survive me, then unto his son JUNIUS SPENCER MORGAN, Junior, desiring, however, that the legatee thereof should divide such of them as he may think proper among my sons-in-law and my friends.

So that none of Morgan's other relatives got their noses out of joint, Morgan's Will includes the following:

> It is not from any lack of affection or regard for them that this will contains no provision for my sisters Sarah Spencer Morgan, Mary Lyman Burns and Juliet Pierpont Morgan, but only because the property which they already have makes the same seem unnecessary.

Of course, another million or two would not have hurt . . . .

There were several other individual bequests in the Will, and every employee of J. P. Morgan & Co. was reportedly given an extra year's salary. Not bad for a bank job. There were also a $500,000 bequest to St. George's Church and $100,000 each to the Episcopal diocese and the House of Rest for Consumptives.

The balance of the estate, estimated at over $100 million, including the art collection, went entirely to J. P.'s son, John, who took over the helm of the great banking house. Compared to the other millionaires of his day such as Rockefeller, Carnegie, Mellon, or Frick, Morgan left a relatively modest estate. That has been attributed to his generosity during his life and the expensive collection of art that he had amassed. A fragment of that collection can be seen today in the magnificent Morgan Library collection in Morgan's former home at Thirty-sixth street and Madison Avenue in New York.

/S/ *John Pierpont Morgan*

WILL DATED: January 4, 1913

Howard Hughes

Date and Place of Birth	Date and Place of Death
December 24, 1905 Houston, Texas	April 5, 1976 In a Learjet flying over Texas

Summa, but Not Loud

Reclusive and mysterious Howard Hughes had an estate estimated to be worth in excess of $1.5 billion when he died in 1976. Hughes's great empire had rapidly grown from the time he began to direct his family's company, Hughes Tool Company, at the age of eighteen after his mother died. At his death, Hughes had parlayed the Hughes Tool Company into the billion-dollar-plus "Summa Corporation," which was Hughes's personal holding company controlling the bulk of his vast assets. Summa controlled his radio and television stations, his architecture and design firm, his string of gold mines, and all the rest of Hughes's multifarious playthings.

Part of Hughes's vast fortune was accumulated through his ownership of the Hughes Aircraft Company. Later in his career, Hughes was the majority owner of Trans World Airlines, selling his interest for $566 million in the 1960s. Hughes was also associated with aircraft by the records he set flying planes. It is therefore ironic that it was ultimately on an airplane in flight from Acapulco to the Methodist Hospital in the city of his birth, Houston, on which the aviational phenomenon died from an illness that is still shrouded in mystery.

In addition to his aircraft-related investments, Hughes also owned substantial real estate and hotels in Las Vegas, Nevada, where he was domiciled when he died. In Las Vegas, Hughes was the owner of the Desert Inn, the Sands, the Silver Slipper, and the Castaway hotels, in addition to a huge ranch and a small airport. Earlier in his career, Hughes had dabbled in films and opened his own movie studio in Hollywood.

During the later part of his life, Hughes was reported to be obsessed with his privacy. He usually traveled in the dead of night and allowed himself to be seen only by a few of his closest advisers, preferring to shield himself behind telephone lines controlling his international business network.

Hughes had been divorced from his first wife, Ella Rice, in 1928 after four years of marriage. Hughes's second marriage, to Jean Peters, lasted from 1957 until ending in divorce in 1971. Besides his wives, only a few trusted advisers ever got close to the mystery man.

One close Hughes adviser described Hughes's concerns about the secrecy surrounding his Will as follows: "The industrialist had different secretaries type different pages and had several different versions typed. Then he could go in a closet, shuffle the papers together from different versions, and burn the pages he didn't want to use, and nobody would have the slightest idea what he wanted to do with his money." If Hughes intended to obfuscate his wishes regarding the distribution of his estate, he succeeded.

The legal controversy surrounding Howard Hughes's purported Last Will and Testament has probably never been rivaled. Over thirty different versions of Hughes's purported Will were submitted to the Nevada, California, and Texas probate courts, and all wanted a piece of the huge Hughes property pie. Following are only three of the purported Hughes Wills submitted to the courts, including the most famous, the "Melvin Dummar/Mormon Church" version.

The first purported Will was allegedly handwritten by Hughes. Under this Will the entire Hughes estate was left to the Howard Hughes Medical Institute (HHMI), which Hughes had established in 1953.

Jan. 11/72

This is my Last Will and Testament

(1) I hereby revoke all Wills and testamentary dispositions of every nature or kind whatsoever made by me before this date.

(2) I nominate, constitute, and appoint my counsel Chester C. Davis, sole executor and trustee of this, my Last Will and Testament....

(3) I give, devise, and bequeath all my monies, holdings, property of every nature and kind, all of my possessions and any profits of the before mentioned to the Howard Hughes Medical Institute for the use of medical research and the betterment of medical and health standards around the world.

(4) I hereby direct my trustee Chester Davis and my assistants Nadine Henley and Frank Gay to continue in their positions and duties, and to also assume a controlling interest in management in the Medical Institute, to decide, direct and implement policies and funds for the proper uses of the Medical Institute in the areas of medical research and the betterment of world health and medical standards.

(5) I hereby request that my trustee make known to any business associates, aides, or confidantes who wish to, or have undertaken a written documentation of any or all parts of my life, the terms of the Rosemont Enterprises agreement and possible infringements thereof—because of the conditions of that document.

(6) I hereby direct my trustee to instruct Rosemont Enterprises to complete all written, visual, and audio, documentation in the presentation of the fac-

tual representation of my life for public release two
years to the day, after my death.

(7) I authorize my trustee to make funds available limited to one quarter of the total estate to a private
agency of my trustee's choice, in the event of my
death by unnatural or man-made cause; to appre-
hend such person or group of persons and to bring
them within full prosecution of the law; the funds
being made available for legal expenses and costs
incurred on behalf of the trustee's appointed
agency.

(8) I wish to make known to my trustee that I did not
at any time enter into any contracts, agreements,
or promises either oral or written, that transferred
gave or bequeathed the bulk or any part of my estate to any person, persons, organizations or whatever other than the Howard Hughes Medical
Institute. I sign this as my Last Will and Testament.

/S/ *Howard R. Hughes*
Jan. 11, 1972

Although the HHMI Will was not admitted to probate, we
need not be concerned about the plight of the HHMI. Shortly
after he established it in 1953, Hughes transferred all of his
assets in the tremendous Hughes Aircraft Company into the
name of the HHMI. That gift made the HHMI one of the
most well-endowed medical centers in the country, and it still
is today.

According to this next purported Will, "Richard Robard
Hughes, aka Joseph Michael Brown," was to inherit the entire
estate:

LAST WILL AND TESTAMENT
OF
HOWARD ROBARD HUGHES JR.

I, Howard Robard Hughes, being of sound mind and body do hereby declare this my Last Will and Testament. I leave my entire estate to my son, Richard Robard Hughes, aka Joseph Michael Brown, born September 12th, 1945 in Fort Worth, Texas. At this time, I plan to make public my son's existence but in the event I am unable to do that, this will cancel and supercede any previous Wills that I have made in the past. By the time this would be read attorneys for Summa Corporation should have approached my son but in the event that has not been done my son should request a full accounting of all my holdings and should take full control thereof.

/S/ *Howard R. Hughes*
April 11, 1975 Las Vegas, Nevada

Good luck, Joseph Michael Brown. It is of course highly unlikely that a man with the great resources and access to legal expertise of Howard Hughes would have resorted to such a crude Will as the foregoing. It is perhaps for that reason that this Will was never admitted to probate.

Finally, there is the famous "Melvin Dummar/Mormon Church" version of the Hughes last Will, which was portrayed in the film *Melvin and Howard*. The film starred Jason Robards as a very scraggly Howard Hughes, who is picked up after a motorcycle accident by a young trucker named Melvin Dummar, and the rest was mystery. According to this version of the Will, Dummar was to inherit one-sixteenth of the Hughes estate, valued at $156 million. Unfortunately for Melvin, that Will was not admitted to probate either. According to the movie *Melvin and Howard*, Dummar was last seen driving a Coors beer delivery truck out west. In light of his experience, one wonders whether Dummar is still willing to pick up scraggly-looking hitchhikers.

I Howard R. Hughes being of sound and disposing mind and memory, not acting under duress, fraud or other undue influence of any person whomsoever, and being a resident of Las Vegas, Nevada declare that this is to be my Last Will and revoke all other Wills previously made by me.

After my death my estate is to be divided as follows:

first: one forth of all my assets to go to "Hughes Medical Institute of Miami.

second: one eight of assets to be divided among the University of Texas—Rice Institute of Technology of Houston—the University of Nevada and the University of Calif.

third: one sixteenth to Church of Jesus Christ of Latterday Saints—David O. Makay

Forth: one sixteenth to establish a home for Orphan Children

Fifth: one sixteenth of assets to go to Boy Scouts of America

sixth: one sixteenth to be divided among Jean Peters of Los Angeles and Ella Rice of Houston

seventh: one sixteenth of assets to William R. Loomis of Houston, Texas

eighth: one sixteenth to go to Melvin DuMar of Gabbs, Nevada

ninth: one sixteenth to be divided among my personal aids at the time of my death

tenth: one sixteenth to be used as school scholarship fund for entire country the spruce goose is to be given to the City of Long Beach, Calif.

the remainder of My estate is to be divided among the key men of the companys I own at the time of my death

I appoint Noah Dietrich as the executor of this Will

signed the 19 day of March 1968

/S/ *Howard R. Hughes*

This last purported Will is not exactly a model of clarity, good grammar, or correct spelling. It does however make provisions for Hughes's famed airplane, the "Spruce Goose." Nonetheless, it is hard to imagine how anyone could expect a competent court to accept this as the worldly billionaire's last Will. Nonetheless, it was only after a lengthy court battle that this Will was finally rejected in the courts and Melvin went truckin' again, all his chips cashed in.

In the end, after lengthy trials and hearings none of the foregoing Wills or any of the other Wills submitted to the Nevada court were admitted to probate. The great Hughes estate passed by intestacy to various distant Hughes relatives with whom the reclusive billionaire had had little or no contact during his lifetime. By his failure to make and/or leave a valid Will, the Hughes estate passed to many "laughing heirs," and Uncle Sam was also able to reap more than a fair share. Perhaps the great brouhaha over his Will and estate would have made the litigious but secretive Hughes proud, but failing to leave his estate to medical research as he had often indicated as his desire cost his estate hundreds of millions of dollars in unnecessary taxes. That is enough to turn anyone over in his grave.

/S/ *Howard R. Hughes*

J. Paul Getty

Date and Place of Birth	Date and Place of Death
December 15, 1892 Minneapolis, Minnesota	June 6, 1976 Sutton Place Surrey, England

Why Not to Marry a Billionaire

For many years described as "the richest man in the world," J. Paul Getty died in 1976 with an estate worth in excess of $2 billion. The bulk of his estate was the value of the over 12 million shares of the Getty Oil Company stock that he controlled through his personal ownership or by the Sarah Getty Trust, of which he was the sole beneficiary. Getty also owned a fabulous mansion called Sutton Place outside London, which was situated on over seven hundred acres of land, had its own private trout stream, and included over thirty cottages and lodges on the property. Sutton Place housed much of the great Getty art and furniture collection, which he had acquired over the course of many years with the shrewd advice of art and antique experts. Finally, there was the property located in Malibu, California, which was Getty's legal domicile at the time of his death. That property would later house the wealthiest art museum the world had ever known.

Throughout his life Getty had the reputation of being a womanizer who when he became bored with one playmate would move on to the next. He was married five times. In 1923 at the age of thirty, Getty married eighteen-year-old Jeannette Dumont. They had one child, George Franklin Getty II, and were then divorced in 1925. In 1926, Getty married the daughter of a Texas rancher, Allene Ashby, but they were divorced two years later. Next, Getty married a German fräulein named Adolphine Helmle, and together they had one son, Jean Ronald Getty, before getting divorced in 1932. That same year Getty married his fourth wife, the movie star Ann Rork, with whom he had two children, J. Paul Getty, Jr., and Gordon Peter Getty. J. P. divorced Ann three years later in 1935. Finally, Getty married a cabaret singer named Louise Dudley "Teddy" Lynch, with whom he had one son named Timothy Ware Getty. Timothy died at the age of twelve in 1958, the same year that his parents were divorced. After five strikes at marriage, Getty apparently gave up on matrimony, but not on women. It is interesting to note that only one of his five wives, Teddy, to whom he was wed the longest, is mentioned in his Will; her monthly support payment of $8,333 while Getty was alive was reduced in the Will to $4,583. However, many of Getty's girlfriends received bequests of Getty stock or monthly allowances under his Will. Apparently, a woman could do better financially by *not* marrying the billionaire.

Longtime Getty employees fared better than Getty's ex-wives, but not much. Most of them received bequests equal to a three- or six-month multiple of their respective salaries. One aide who was one of Getty's most trusted advisers received an extra six months pay under the Will, which was reportedly equal to approximately $36,000. Not an amount that someone who worked so closely with the world's richest man would want to write home about.

Getty signed his Will in Italy in 1958 after his last divorce and after the death of his son Timothy. The Getty Will ultimately admitted to probate is most unusual because it has twenty-one codicils, or subsequent amendments, to it. One wonders why a new Will was not prepared after 1958 that would incorporate the changes made up until then. One explanation for this extraordinary use of so many codicils is that

Getty wanted people to know exactly when they had fallen out of his favor.

Getty was known to have stormy relationships with his sons. Their respective shares of his estate shift dramatically over the course of the many changes in the Will. At various points Getty's sons are removed or inserted as executors of the Will or their shares of Getty stock are increased or decreased. For example, in the fifth codicil to the Will, signed in 1963, Getty's youngest son, Gordon, is stripped of his right to share in his father's personal effects and receives a measly bequest of "the sum of Five Hundred Dollars ($500) and nothing else," while the shares of Getty stock given to his brothers George and Paul were doubled. Son Ronald's bequest was left the same. In the fourteenth codicil, signed in 1971, Getty son J. Paul Getty, Jr., joined his brother Gordon in the penalty box and also received only "the sum of Five Hundred Dollars ($500) and nothing else." In the nineteenth codicil, signed in 1975, son Gordon comes back into favor and becomes an executor and trustee of the Will with his brother Ronnie. Son Paul remained in the Getty penalty box.

Getty signed the twenty-first and last codicil to his Will in March of 1976, a few months before he died. In that last codicil, Getty turned control of the Getty Museum's Getty Oil Company stock over to the museum's board of trustees, which was not controlled by Getty-family members. By bequeathing most of his estate to the charitable museum, Getty was able to avoid huge estate taxes by virtue of the unlimited charitable deduction then in effect. Furthermore, Getty created an eternal monument to his name by creating the most richly endowed museum the world had ever known. By the time the Getty estate was distributed, the museum's endowment was greater than $1 billion. The annual income on that amount alone was significantly more than that available to any other museum in the world.

The Getty Museum in Malibu overlooking the Pacific Ocean

was also intended to be Getty's final resting place. One of the first articles of Getty's 1958 Will states:

> (a) I give and devise unto my Executors and Trustees ... such portion of my ranch property located at 17985 Pacific Coast Highway, Pacific Palisades, California, not in excess of one (1) acre, as they, in their discretion, may deem appropriate for the erection thereon of a suitable small, marble mausoleum to receive my mortal remains and those of such of my sons and their respective wives and issue as shall choose to be interred therein, together with a right or easement of access thereto over or through the balance of my said ranch property.
>
> (b) I give and bequeath to my said Executors and Trustees such sum, not in excess of Fifty Thousand Dollars ($50,000), as they in their discretion shall deem necessary or desirable for the purpose of erecting such mausoleum, and I direct that they cause such mausoleum to be so erected.
>
> (c) I give and bequeath to my said Executors and Trustees the further sum of One Hundred Thousand Dollars ($100,000), IN TRUST ... to apply the same and so much of the principal thereof as may be necessary to the perpetual maintenance and care of said mausoleum and the land upon which the same is erected.

Evidently, Getty's final resting place was important to him, but after his body was flown from England to California, it was discovered that none of Getty's expensive lawyers or anyone else had ever obtained the proper permits for Getty to be buried on his private property. Getty's body was kept embalmed and refrigerated at the Forest Lawn Memorial Park in Glendale for almost three years after his death until a variance in the California law could be obtained that would allow him to be buried on the property that he loved so dearly. Even the richest man in this world needed the proper paperwork before he could make his way to the next.

/S/ Jean Paul Getty

WILL DATED: September 22, 1958
1ST CODICIL: June 18, 1960
2ND CODICIL: November 4, 1962
3RD CODICIL: December 20, 1962
4TH CODICIL: January 15, 1963
5TH CODICIL: March 6, 1963
6TH CODICIL: September 16, 1965
7TH CODICIL: March 11, 1966
8TH CODICIL: January 5, 1967
9TH CODICIL: November 3, 1967
10TH CODICIL: February 24, 1969
11TH CODICIL: March 28, 1969
12TH CODICIL: June 26, 1970
13TH CODICIL: March 8, 1971
14TH CODICIL: July 29, 1971
15TH CODICIL: March 20, 1973
16TH CODICIL: June 14, 1973
17TH CODICIL: October 9, 1973
18TH CODICIL: July 4, 1974
19TH CODICIL: January 21, 1975
20TH CODICIL: August 27, 1975
21ST CODICIL: March 11, 1976

Conrad Hilton

Date and Place of Birth

December 25, 1887
Territory of New Mexico

Date and Place of Death

January 3, 1979
St. John's Hospital
Santa Monica, California

No More Room Service

Hilton Hotel chain founder Conrad Nicholson Hilton came from humble beginnings when he was born on Christmas Day to a Norwegian immigrant family in the Territory of New Mexico. Hilton's father ran a $2.50-a-night boardinghouse in the little town where they lived. Conrad, who was the second of eight children, rose to be the chairman of the prestigious Hilton Hotel chain in nineteen countries around the world. Hilton was known to be a tireless worker, putting in six days a week well into his late eighties.

As evidenced by his Will, Hilton was also a profoundly religious man. Perhaps Hilton felt that because he was born on December 25, he also had a special mission to fulfill. As his Will states to the directors and trustees of the Conrad N. Hilton Foundation:

> I bequeath some cherished conclusions formed during a lifetime of observation, study and contemplation:
>
> There is a natural law, a Divine law, that obliges you and me to relieve the suffering, the distressed and the destitute. Charity is a supreme virtue, and the great channel through which the mercy of God is passed on to mankind. It is the virtue that unites men and inspires their noblest efforts.

"Love one another, for that is the whole law"; so our fellowmen deserve to be loved and encouraged—never to be abandoned to wander alone in poverty and darkness. The practice of charity will bind us,—will bind all men in one great brotherhood.

As the funds you will expend have come from many places in the world, so let there be no territorial, religious, or color restrictions on your benefactions, but beware of organized, professional charities with high-salaried executives and a heavy ratio of expense.

Be ever watchful for the opportunity to shelter little children with the umbrella of your charity; be generous to their schools, their hospitals and their places of worship. For, as they must bear the burdens of our mistakes, so are they in their innocence the repositories of our hopes for the upward progress of humanity. Give aid to their protectors and defenders, the Sisters, who devote their love and life's work for the good of mankind for they appeal especially to me as being deserving of help from the FOUNDATION. I know the SISTERS OF LORETTO very well, as it was this order who first established educational institutions in my home state of New Mexico. I have had an opportunity of observing the fine work they do. The SISTERS OF THE SACRED HEART is another order that I have assisted in Chicago, but there are many deserving support in other fields, particularly hospitals. Deserving charities exist everywhere, but it is manifest that you cannot help all; so, it is my wish, without excluding others, to have the largest part of your benefactions dedicated to the Sisters in all parts of the world.

Besides having a soft spot for the Sisters, Conrad Hilton also had three wives. With his first wife, Mary Barron, he had three sons—William Barron Hilton, Eric Michael Hilton, and Conrad Nicholson, Jr. (Conrad "Nicky" Hilton, Jr., was once married to Elizabeth Taylor and died in 1969 at the age of forty-two.) After Conrad and Mary were divorced, Hilton married Zsa Zsa Gabor, with whom he had a daughter named Constance Francesca. After his divorce from Zsa Zsa (a/k/a Sari), Hilton married Frances Kelly when he was eighty-nine years old. The papers filed with the Los Angeles court state that Conrad Hilton and Frances Kelly had entered into a written antenuptial agreement "in contemplation of marriage" that provided for the lifetime support of Frances Kelly and in which she "relinquished, disclaimed, released and forever gave up any and all rights, claims or interest in or to" Hilton's property.

As a result of this antenuptial agreement, Hilton had no reason to change his 1973 Will after his 1976 marriage. In his 1973 Will Hilton described his family as follows:

> FIRST: I declare that I am unmarried. I further declare that I have been duly and legally divorced from my last wife, SARI G. HILTON, and have fully discharged a final property settlement agreement entered into with her.
>
> I have only three living children, namely WILLIAM BARRON HILTON, ERIC MICHAEL HILTON and CONSTANCE FRANCESCA HILTON. As will hereafter appear in this Will, different and unequal bequests have been made to my several children, and I hereby declare this to be my deliberate intention and purpose.

To his two surviving sons, William Barron Hilton and Eric Michael Hilton, Conrad Hilton gave "all of my automobiles, jewelry and personal effects of every kind" to be divided by them as they should agree, or if they failed to agree, then as his executors (William Barron Hilton excluded) should decide. To his son William Barron, who was the president of the Hilton Hotels Corporation when his father died, Conrad gave "shares of stock in Hilton Hotels Corporation and Trans World

Airlines, Inc., or both, in the combined aggregate value of Seven Hundred Fifty Thousand Dollars ($750,000.00)." To his son Eric, who was a divisional vice president of Hilton Inns, Inc. when his father died, Hilton gave "shares of stock in Hilton Hotels Corporation or Trans World Airlines, Inc., or both, in the combined aggregate value of Three Hundred Thousand Dollars ($300,000.00)." It is a good thing that Hilton pointed out at the start that bequests would not be so even among his children. But the bequests to children, employees, and other relatives get even more skewed, as follows:

SIXTH: I hereby make further gifts and bequests as follows...

A. (1) To my daughter, CONSTANCE FRANCESCA HILTON, the sum of One Hundred Thousand Dollars ($100,000.00).

(2) To my sister, HELEN BUCKLEY, of Little Compton, Rhode Island, the sum of Fifty Thousand Dollars ($50,000.00).

(3) To my sister ROSEMARY CARPENTER, of Little Compton, Rhode Island, the sum of Fifty Thousand Dollars ($50,000.00).

...

(16) To my valued friend and administrative assistant, OLIVE M. WAKEMAN, the sum of Seventy-five Thousand Dollars ($75,000.00).

(17) To my valued employee, HUGO MENTZ, the sum of Thirty Thousand Dollars ($30,000.00).

(18) To SISTER FRANCETTA BARBERIS, of Washington, D.C., my star sapphire ring.

(19) To THE CALIFORNIA PROVINCE OF THE SOCIETY OF JESUS... money or assets of the value of One Hundred Thousand Dollars ($100,000.00) in cash or in kind, or partly in cash and partly in kind.

I intentionally make no provision for my sister EVA LEWIS, as she is amply provided for by other means.

Hilton gave the rest of his entire estate, worth over $108 million, according to papers filed with the court, to the "CONRAD N. HILTON FOUNDATION, incorporated in the State of California on or about February 21, 1950 as a charitable corporation." To the directors of the Hilton Foundation, he also gave the words of religious wisdom quoted at the beginning of this subchapter.

For his executors, Hilton named his son William Barron Hilton and his trusted attorney and adviser James E. Bates. The Will states further, "By reason of the size and magnitude of my estate, my Executors . . . are authorized to appoint, upon such terms as they may fix, the BANK OF AMERICA NATIONAL TRUST AND SAVINGS ASSOCIATION . . . as a depository and as an agent or agents for Executors, to assist them in the administration and distribution of my estate." After all, somebody had to do all the paperwork.

As one might expect, there is an *in terrorem* clause in Hilton's Will, but it is unusual in stating that if all his heirs were to contest the Will, and lose, the ultimate beneficiary would be the State of California.

Finally, Hilton requested that he be buried next to his brother, August Harold Hilton, in Dallas, Texas. Hilton's first hotel successes had been in Texas, and it appears that he liked the Texas service.

/S/ Conrad Nicholson Hilton

WILL DATED: October 31, 1973

Nelson A. Rockefeller

Date and Place of Birth	Date and Place of Death
July 8, 1908 Bar Harbour, Maine	January 26, 1979 13 West 54th Street Lenox Hill Hospital New York, New York

Happy in Camp Rockefeller

A grandson of the founder of the Standard Oil Company, which created the vast family fortune, Nelson Aldrich Rockefeller used his immense family wealth to pursue a political career and later to collect and donate works of art worth hundreds of millions of dollars. After the Republican Party lost the White House in the 1976 elections, Rockefeller pulled out of politics and devoted himself to his personal affairs, especially those related to his many works of art. Many provisions of his Will demonstrate the great importance of art in Rockefeller's life, not only as investments, but as objects of beauty to be studied and enjoyed.

A few days after his being graduated from Dartmouth College, Rockefeller married Mary Todhunter Clark. After having five children together, Rockefeller was divorced from Mary in 1962. The divorce occurred shortly after one of the Rockefellers' five children, Michael, was lost on an anthropological expedition in the jungles of New Guinea and later declared dead after a massive search failed to find him. Despite this tragic loss, Rockefeller continued to collect primitive art.

In 1962, Rockefeller married Margaretta Fitler Murphy, nicknamed Happy, five weeks after her own divorce. Happy was nineteen years younger than Nelson, and apparently, she kept him happy. Together, they had two children, Nelson, Jr., who was born in 1964, and Mark, born in 1967. Regarding his second family, Rockefeller states in the preamble of his Will:

> In this Will I make my wife, Margaretta Fitler Rockefeller, my sons Nelson, Jr. and Mark and charity the primary beneficiaries of my estate. I make relatively small provision for my older children, Rodman, Ann, Steven and Mary. I do this because my older children have already been amply provided for by my father, John D. Rockefeller, Jr., and by gifts made by me during my lifetime. Nelson, Jr., and Mark were born after my father's death and do not benefit from his gifts to the same extent as do my older children. Although I have tried to make up for this during my lifetime, a discrepancy in the economic well-being of my two youngest children and my older children still exists. It is for this reason that I make greater provision in this Will for Nelson, Jr. and Mark than I do for my older children.

The Rockefeller family owned land and property all over the globe, and in his Will Nelson gives to his wife:

> 1) all real property owned by me at the time of my death on Mount Desert Island, County of Hancock, State of Maine, together with all buildings thereon and all rights and easements appurtenant to said real property...
> 2) the house designed by Junzo Yoshimura and all of my interest in the house known as the "Hawes" house both of which are located within the area known as the "Park"...in Pocantico Hills, County of Westchester, State of New York....
> 3) the property known as "The Camp" located in Pocantico Hills, Westchester County, New York, which

consists of approximately 147.025 acres of real property, together with all structures located on said real
property, all rights and easements appurtenant to said
structures and said real property and all policies of
insurance relating thereto (hereinafter referred to as
the "Camp property"). To guide my Executors and wife
in the disposition of the Camp property, I am depositing
with my Will a copy of a map which was prepared in
May 1977 by Chas. H. Sells, Inc., which shows the Camp
property and the division of said property into the parcels known as the "outer Camp property" and "inner
Camp property".

Presumably, the "inner" and "outer" camps, the New York
City cooperative apartment located at 812 Fifth Avenue, and
other property left to Mrs. Rockefeller were enough to keep
her happy.

But there was also the 4,180-acre Rockefeller-family estate
in Westchester County, New York, left to Nelson and his
brothers by their father, John D. Rockefeller, Jr. The disposition of this historic property required special consideration under Rockefeller's Will.

The Will makes detailed provisions for the disposition of
Rockefeller's enormous art collection. From his primitive art
collection, Rockefeller gave 1,610 items, which were all listed
in the Will by their Rockefeller-collection catalogue number,
to the Metropolitan Museum of Art in New York. This bequest
was certainly fitting, as young Nelson had become a member
of the Metropolitan Museum's Board of Directors the year he
was graduated from college. Today, the Rockefeller collection
of primitive art occupies an entire wing of that museum.

To the Museum of Modern Art, of which he had been the
president in 1939, Rockefeller bequeathed many modern
paintings, including important works by Picasso, Matisse, and
Calder.

Rockefeller left his collection of oriental sculpture located on the property called Eyrie Garden, which he owned in Mount Desert Island, Maine, "to such one or more of the United States of America, any State or a political subdivision thereof, in all cases for exclusively public purposes." It seems oddly appropriate in the light of the later sale of Rockefeller Center to a Japanese company that the United States public should have been left "Rocky's" oriental sculpture collection.

After disposing of the larger art collections, the Will provides:

> All paintings, pieces of sculpture and other objects of art, all furniture, furnishings, rugs, pictures, books, silver, plate, linen, china, glassware, jewelry, wearing apparel, automobiles and their accessories, including antique automobiles, boats and their accessories, and all other household and personal goods and effects...

should be given to the charity taking the real properties where this tangible property was located, or to Mrs. Rockefeller, or to the two younger Rockefeller children if she did not survive. Other tangible property with a value not to exceed $25,000 (which was originally $100,000 in the Will) was to be selected by *each* of Rockefeller's six children and Happy's daughter from her prior marriage.

In addition to the real estate, artworks, Rockefeller's personal papers, and other tangible property left to Happy, she also received an amount equal to approximately one-half of Nelson's "adjusted gross estate," which was, of course, quite substantial.

There were no other gifts to individuals under the Will other than the following provision found under lucky article thirteen of the Will:

> I release and discharge each of Susan Cable Herter, Megan R. Marshack and Hugh Morrow from any indebtedness, including interest thereon, which he or she may

owe to me at the time of my death, and I direct my
Executors to cancel any promissory notes or other evidence of his or her indebtedness to me.

Morrow, Herter, and Marshack were all associates and friends
of Rockefeller. The amount of Marshack's forgiven debt to
Rockefeller was reportedly $45,000, which he had loaned her
to purchase a cooperative apartment near the town house
where she was with Rockefeller on the night he died.

It has widely been reported that the thirty-one-year-old
Marshack was working with Rockefeller on a book about his
art collection when he suffered a heart attack at approximately
10:15 P.M. on the night he died. The police reported that the
first call for emergency help came in at 11:16 P.M.; the delay
in reporting the attack has never been explained. The first
reports of Rockefeller's death stated that he was working at
his Rockefeller Center office on the night he died. Later reports corrected that and placed him at the town house he
owned at 13 West Fifty-fourth Street. Ms. Marshack reportedly lived at 25 West Fifty-fourth Street. Whether Rockefeller's death was attributable to low blood pressure—70 over
31—has long been a matter of ribald speculation. Family
spokesman Hugh Morrow was quoted in *The New York Times*
as saying about Rockefeller's death, "He was having a won-
derful time with the whole art enterprise. He was 'having a
ball,' as he put it."

When he died, Rockefeller was survived by two of his five
siblings, David and Laurance. For his executors and trustees,
Rockefeller named his brother Laurance and two longtime
advisers, J. Richardson Dilworth and Donal C. O'Brien, Jr.
Conspicuously absent from Nelson's nominated group of executors was his brother David, who was the chairman of the
Chase Manhattan Bank. Perhaps Nelson did not want a banker
on the team. But Nelson's own shrewdness is shown by the
clause pertaining to executor's commissions requiring that
brother Laurance waive all his executor's commissions due to

him pursuant to New York law and that the other two named executors accept commissions in an amount agreed to with Laurance. The commissions to each executor of an estate the size of Rockefeller's would have been millions of dollars. Certainly brother Laurance did not need any more taxable income, and perhaps Nelson believed the money better spent by passing it to the next Rockefeller generation to inherit his philanthropic mantle.

/S/ *Nelson A. Rockefeller*

WILL DATED: December 6, 1978

Malcolm Forbes

Date and Place of Birth	Date and Place of Death
August 19, 1919 Englewood, New Jersey	February 24, 1990 Timberfield Far Hills, New Jersey

He Went Thataway . . .

M(B)illionaire Malcolm Forbes certainly knew how to live it up. He owned eight homes around the world ranging from his forty wooded acres and mansion in Far Hills, New Jersey, to his private island of Lauthala in the Fiji Islands. Forbes could travel to his various properties either on his 151-foot yacht called the *Highlander*, on his private 727 jet called *Capitalist Tool*, on any of his many motorbikes, or up, up, and away in one of his beautiful fleet of hot-air balloons. At home, Forbes could toy with one of his twelve Russian Imperial Fabergé eggs or his armies of tin soldiers or rare books and famous autographs. If it is true that "He who dies with the most toys, wins," then Malcolm Forbes had to be near the top of the heap. By the way, during business hours, Forbes ran a little magazine bearing his name. Somehow, despite a fortune variously estimated between $400,000 and $1.25 billion, his name managed to evade *Forbes* magazine's annual list of the richest four hundred. Editor in chief's prerogative.

Forbes's sixty-one-page Will lives up to his reputation for being a generous man with rich and eclectic tastes. Forbes proves his gastronomic and epicurean bent by making $1,000 bequests to each of the proprietors of nine of New York City's best restaurants "as a token of gratitude for the joy their skills and genius added to the lives of those who've been lucky and

259

sensible enough to dine at their restaurants." The proprietors and restaurants making the Forbes favorite nine were the following: Paul C. Kovi and Tom G. Margittai of The Four Seasons, André Soltner of Lutèce, Giselle Masson and Charles Masson of La Grenouille, David and Karen Waltuck of Chanterelle, Sirio Maccioni of Le Cirque, Roberto Ruggeri of Bice, Nobuyoshi Kuraoka of Nippon, Rocky Akoi of Benihana, and Glenn Bernbaum of Mortimer's.

Following those gastronomic bequests, Forbes shifts gears and makes $1,000 bequests to almost thirty different "Motorcycle Clubs . . . whose Sunday runs provided so much pleasure and fellowship for me and so many other cycling enthusiasts." The names of these clubs ranged from Heavy Metal, of Newark, New Jersey, to the Blue Knights II, of the Bronx, New York. Forbes also made a $10,000 bequest to the American Motorcyclist Association, located in Westerville, Ohio.

In his Will Forbes rewards a few of his Far Hills, New Jersey, neighbors and "dear friends, as token compensation for the bridge (and other) lessons they've so generously, warmly and patiently given me over the years." One has to wonder what "other" types of lessons were so "warmly . . . given." Next Forbes makes two $10,000 bequests to two "treasured" friends, one of Washington, D.C., and the other, Countess Boul De Breteuil of Marrakech-Guleiz, Morocco. After those cash bequests to six friends, the Will section concludes:

> All other friends, family, employees and favored Causes
> (in most instances, they each are all of the foregoing)
> I've taken care of either in life or by other means after
> my "cease-and-desisting."

If anyone out there can explain exactly what Forbes meant by his "cease-and-desisting," please let the author know.

In 1985, Forbes had been divorced from his wife of thirty-nine years, the former Roberta Remsen Laidlaw. Pursuant to a "Property Settlement Agreement" that the Forbeses signed in 1985, there is a $5-million bequest "to my former wife, Roberta L. Forbes." In addition she is entitled to payments from the Forbes estate of $4,000 per week. There is a $2-million bequest to Forbes's daughter, Moira F. Mumma (which would have been $5 million if former wife Roberta had not survived Forbes).

Forbes seemed to believe in the Anglo-Saxon tradition of primogeniture, in which the eldest son in a family received most if not all of his ancestor's estate. True to his Scottish form, Forbes made son Malcolm S. Forbes, Jr., the controlling heir by giving him a 51-percent voting interest in Forbes Inc. stock. The remaining stock is divided equally among the remaining Forbes children. After Forbes's death, the children appeared harmonious, so there must have been enough to keep everyone happy.

All the rest of Forbes's multivaried tangible property is divided among his five children. Forbes's residuary estate is devised and bequeathed to such of his descendants as survived him, *"per stirpes*, or, if none, in equal shares to such of the spouses of my deceased children as shall survive me." It is interesting that Forbes chose to mention the spouses of his children as possible residuary beneficiaries in the unlikely event that all of Forbes's descendants were deceased. Nonetheless, it is unusual to see spouses of children mentioned in that context. After all, Forbes could have chosen to name one of his favorite motorcycle clubs as the taker in the case of a Forbes family disaster.

In line with the concept of primogeniture, Forbes named his son Malcolm S. Forbes, Jr., as the sole executor of and trustee under his Will. If son Malcolm, Jr., ceased to act, then Timothy C., Christopher C., and Robert L., in the order named according to the Will, are designated as the successor to their brother. Youngest daughter Moira is not named as a fiduciary in the Will.

Despite his dramatic and high-flying lifestyle, Malcolm Forbes died mundanely—in his sleep in his bed in his primary home in Far Hills, New Jersey. Earlier that morning, Forbes had returned home from London aboard his private jet after playing in an international corporate bridge tournament. Forbes directed that he be cremated and that his ashes be buried on his private Fiji island, Lauthala. He further directed that the epitaph on his grave read simply, "WHILE ALIVE, HE LIVED." Dead at three score and ten, Malcolm Forbes had certainly led the richest of lives and definitely enjoyed himself before he experienced "life's only certainty."

/S/ *Malcolm S. Forbes*

WILL DATED: July 8, 1988

END NOTES

"Let's Choose Executors and
Talk of Wills"
—Shakespeare

End Notes

"Let's choose Executors and talk of Wills"
—Shakespeare, *King Richard II*

A brief bit of historical and legal background might be helpful here. The foreboding-sounding term *Last Will and Testament* is a creation of archaic legal scholars with names such as Blackstone, Kent, and Coke. During Anglo-Saxon times, the word *Will* applied to the disposition of only land, or "real" property, and the word *testament* applied to the disposition of only "personal" property, such as cattle, corporate stock, or cash. With the passage of the English Statute of Wills in 1837, the distinction between a Will and testament was formally abolished, and thereafter any and all property, real or personal, passed by one unified document, a decedent's "Last Will and Testament." Throughout this volume, we have taken twentieth-century license and referred to a "Last Will and Testament" simply as a "Will." Of course, all of the Wills excerpted within were the decedents' *last* Wills, as determined by the court where the Will was admitted to probate.

After a decedent's original Will (or a copy under certain circumstances if the original cannot be found, as was the case in the estate of Ricky Nelson) has been located, the person or institution named in the Will to execute the Will's directions (appropriately called the executor or executors) offers the Will to a "surrogate's court" or a "probate court" where the decedent had his domicile (i.e., his primary legal residence) for the Will to be "admitted to probate." If no one who has "standing" to object to the admission of the Will objects to its admission and wins, and the court accepts the validity of the Will, the propounded instrument is deemed by the court to be the legally binding Will of the decedent. After the Will has been admitted to probate, the court will issue "letters testamentary" to the person or institution designated as executor of the Will and who agrees to serve in that capacity. He, she, or it then becomes the legal representative of the estate and assumes a host of "fiduciary" duties.

To briefly and generally summarize the duties of an executor, after marshaling and valuing all of the decedent's assets, the executor pays all of the decedent's debts and liabilities. In addition, the executor must pay the taxes and estate administration expenses, including legal and accounting fees and executor's commissions. After making these payments, the executor distributes the balance of the estate in accordance with the testator's directions.

A person metamorphoses into an "estate" upon his or her death. Usually, the estate is distributed and administered in accordance with the deceased person's directions as expressed in his or her Will and in accordance with applicable federal and state law.

After the Internal Revenue Service and the state taxing authorities have finally determined and accepted the tax payments made and a "closing" or "no tax" letter has been received by the executor, the estate can then be wound up or terminated. As simple as it may sound, an estate administration can continue for years, and many estates linger on forever and are never formally or finally wound up. Any trust established under a Will may continue long after the estate has been closed and be administered by the designated trustees in accordance with the terms of that particular trust. Many of the Wills contained in this volume include trust provisions for a surviving spouse, parents, children, grandchildren, or other friends or lovers.

The Terrorizing *in Terrorem Clause*

Many of the Wills excerpted here include the ultimate grave-yard stick, an *in terrorem* clause. *In terrorem* is Latin for "in fright or terror" as a result of a threat. An *in terrorem* clause in a Will threatens the forfeiture of a beneficiary's bequest or interest under the Will should that beneficiary contest the validity of the Will—and lose. These terrorizing clauses are generally drawn quite broadly to apply to anyone who directly or indirectly contests the Will. An *in terrorem* clause is included in a Will when a problem with a beneficiary is foreseen. To be most effective as a threat, the person possibly raising any objections to the Will must have received something of some value under the Will, forcing him or her to think twice before "risking it all" to try for a larger pot of gold. The following rather comprehensive clause is excerpted from the Will of comedian Groucho Marx:

> If any devisee, legatee or beneficiary under this will, or any person claiming under or through any devisee, legatee or beneficiary, or any person who would be entitled to share in my estate through inheritance or intestate succession, or any of my ex-wives [emphasis added], their heirs, successors and assigns, shall, in any manner whatsoever, directly or indirectly, contest this will or attack, oppose or in any manner seek to impair or invalidate any provision hereof, or shall in any manner whatsoever conspire or cooperate with any person or persons attempting to do any of the acts or things aforesaid, or shall acquiesce in or fail to oppose such proceedings (all such persons being herein included within the word "contestant(s)") then in each of the above mentioned cases, I hereby bequeath to such contestant or contestants the sum of $1.00 only, and no more, in lieu of any other bequests, devises and interests

given in this will or inuring to the benefit of such contestant or contestants, and such devises, bequests or interests shall instead be given to THE JEWISH FEDERATION COUNCIL OF GREATER LOS ANGELES. If as a result of any attack or contest of this Will an intestacy would otherwise result as to all or any portion of my estate, then, and in such event, with respect to any such portion of my estate I hereby give, devise and bequeath such portion of my estate to THE JEWISH FEDERATION COUNCIL OF GREATER LOS ANGELES. For the purpose of this Article, an action for declaratory relief or petition for instructions or any other action or proceeding shall be deemed to constitute an attack upon this Will where the purpose of the institution of such action or proceeding would be to oppose, impair or invalidate any provision hereof.

It is indeed ironic that the *in terrorem* clause appears unusually frequently in the Wills of our group "The Comedians." Perhaps our funnymen saw the use of an *in terrorem* clause in their Wills as a way of getting the last laugh on anyone who chose to question their wisdom after they were no longer around to personally defend themselves.

Where There's No Will, There Was No Will . . .

When a person dies without a valid Will, he or she has died "intestate." Despite the many important and emotional benefits derived from having an up-to-date Will, many wealthy, well-educated, and famous people have died without having valid Wills.

The list of those dying intestate must be headed by President Abraham Lincoln. Lincoln's failure to have a Will is unforgivable because he was also one of the leading lawyers of his day. But doesn't "Honest" Abe, the lawyer from Illinois, deserve the benefit of the doubt on this one? Maybe his hiding place for his Will was *too* private and it was just never located. Lincoln is joined on the presidential intestacy parade by Ulysses S. Grant, James Garfield, and Andrew Johnson. Therefore, George, Ron, Jimmy, Jerry, and Dick, if you are still out there, please be sure that your Wills are valid and can be located by your heirs.

Other well-known persons dying intestate include close-to-the-edge comic Lenny Bruce, actor Sal Mineo, actress Jayne Mansfield, designer Willi Smith (despite his first name), and artist Pablo Picasso. Songwriter George Gershwin died a very wealthy man, but with no Will. Gershwin's entire estate was inherited by his mother, Rose Gershwin. Perhaps that is what George wanted. Jazz great Duke Ellington was a Will-less widower, and his entire estate passed to his son, Mercer K. Ellington. Glamorous Hollywood pinup girl Rita Hayworth died without a valid Will. Her daughter, Princess Yasmin Aga Khan, was appointed administrator of her estate by the New York Surrogate's Court. Howard Hughes died intestate because none of his thirty purported Wills were deemed to be valid by the Texas, California, or Nevada courts.

The failure to make a Will may be a person's way of avoiding making binding and immutable decisions involving property, family, and friends, or may be a way of refusing to confront the inevitability of one's death. We have all heard Ben Franklin's often-quoted remark about the twin certainties in life—death and taxes. A Will is designed to address both of those unfortunate realities, but it is often unnerving for the person thinking of signing a Will to do so. In the case of perhaps the wealthiest artist who ever lived, Pablo Picasso (Picasso died with an estate estimated to be worth anywhere between $300 million and $1 billion), his failure to have prepared and signed a Will has been attributed to his superstition that signing his Will would hasten his demise. Perhaps there was something to that, as Picasso was painting until the night he died at the ripe old age of ninety-one. Likewise, one of the shining art stars of the eighties, Jean-Michel Basquiat, also died without a Will. But he was only twenty-seven, so he did not have as much time to contemplate the inevitable as Picasso did. Nonetheless, his Will-less multimillion-dollar estate has engendered nasty litigation that could have been avoided if Basquiat had prepared and signed a proper Will.

Besides all the practical reasons to have a Will, Wills also provide provocative and interesting reading for the curious of the present and future, as we hope has been the case with the Wills assembled here.

Reproductions of Telltale Signatures and Interesting Wills

Georgia O'Keeffe
Robert Mapplethorpe
Alfred J. Hitchcock

The signatures of Georgia O'Keeffe, Robert Mapplethorpe, and Alfred J. Hitchcock reproduced here manifest the ravages of old age, AIDS, and other illness on these three great artists.

IN WITNESS WHEREOF, I have hereunto set my hand this 2' day of August, 1979.

Georgia O'Keeffe

Georgia O'Keeffe

FOURTH: As thus amended, I hereby ratify, confirm, redeclare and republish my said Will.

IN WITNESS WHEREOF, I, GEORGIA O'KEEFFE, have hereunto subscribed my name and affixed my seal this 2 day of November, 1983.

Georgia O'Keeffe

Georgia O'Keeffe

TWELFTH: Except as hereinabove amended, I hereby ratify, confirm and republish my aforesaid Last Will and Testament and prior Codicils thereto.

IN WITNESS WHEREOF, I have hereunto set my hand this 8th day of August, 1984.

Georgia O'Keeffe

GEORGIA O'KEEFFE

WE, the undersigned, do hereby certify that GEORGIA O'KEEFFE, on the day of the date hereof, in our presence, being in the presence of each other, signed, published and declared the above instrument as and to be her Second Codicil to her Last Will and Testament, and that we, on the same occasion, at her request, in her presence, and in the presence of each other, have hereunto signed our names as attesting witnesses.

WITNESS WHEREOF, I have hereunto set my hand and

23 day of June , 1988.

_____ (L.S.)
Robert Mapplethorpe

FIRST CODICIL TO WILL
OF ROBERT MAPPLETHORPE

I hereby amend my will dated June 23, 1988 by directing
my executor to make the following bequests (in addition to any
other bequests made in my said will):

$2,500 to TOM PETERMAN;

$2,500 to MICHAEL LUCINE; and

$5,000 to IRIS OWEN.

In all other respects I hereby ratify and reaffirm all
of the provisions of my will dated June 23, 1988.

IN WITNESS WHEREOF, I have on March 7 , 1989 signed,
sealed, published and declared the foregoing instrument as a First
Codicil to my Last Will and Testament dated June 23, 1988.

_____ (L.S.)

The foregoing instrument was on said date signed,
sealed, published and declared by said ROBERT
MAPPLETHORPE, as said Testator's Codicil to his
Last Will and Testament dated June 23, 1988.

other respects distribution shall be made hereunder as
if my said wife had predeceased me.

IN WITNESS WHEREOF, I have hereunto set my hand
this 8th day of August , 1963, at 10957
Bellagio Rd. Los Angeles 24.

ALFRED J. HITCHCOCK

The foregoing instrument, consisting of
twenty-five (25) pages, including this
page, was upon the date therein named in
our presence and in the presence of each
of us, signed by ALFRED J. HITCHCOCK,
the testator therein named, and published
and declared by him to us and to each of
us to be his Last Will, and we, and each
of us, thereupon at his request and in
his presence and in the presence of each
other have hereunto set our hands as
witnesses thereto. And we and each of
us declare that we believe said testator
to be of sound mind and memory and not
to be acting under duress, menace, fraud
or undue influence of any person or persons
whomsoever.

residing at 146 Central Park C

should for any reason be or become unwilling or
unable so to serve and if my said daughter shall
request the appointment of a co-Trustee hereunder,
then I appoint the BANK OF AMERICA NATIONAL TRUST &
SAVINGS ASSOCIATION as sole Trustee (or as co-Trustee)
of each and every trust created hereunder."

VIII

I hereby revoke subparagraph 3 of Paragraph VI of my
said Last Will and substitute the following therefor:

"3. No bond or other security shall be required
of any of the persons named in subparagraph 1 of this
Paragraph VI as Trustee or co-Trustee hereunder."

IX

I hereby ratify, approve and confirm my said Last Will,
as modified by my First, Second, Third, Fourth and Fifth Codicils
thereto, in all other respects.

IN WITNESS WHEREOF, I have hereunto set my hand
this   day of *March*, 1980, at Los Angeles, California.
   25

_____
ALFRED J. HITCHCOCK

The foregoing instrument, consisting of six (6) pages,
including the following page, was upon the date therein
named in our presence, and in the presence of each of us,
signed by ALFRED J. HITCHCOCK, the testator therein named,
and published and declared by him to us and to each of us
to be the Sixth Codicil to his Last Will, and we, and each
of us, thereupon at his request and in his presence and in
the presence of each other have hereunto set our hands as

The following Will excerpts with signatures reproduced here reveal some of the most intimate and personal feelings of this mixed bag of famous personalities:

Fred Astaire
W. C. Fields
Ricky Nelson
John Lennon
Elvis Presley
Jim Morrison
Cary Grant
Rock Hudson
Joan Crawford
Jean Paul Getty

be paid a reasonable compensation and to be indemnified against all loss, cost or liability in connection with their services. No bond shall be required of any of said trustees, whether acting alone or jointly with other trustees.

EIGHTH: I direct that my funeral be private and that there be no memorial service.

IN WITNESS WHEREOF, I have hereunto set my hand this 6th day of January, 1986, at ___Los Angeles___, California.

Fred Astaire
Fred Astaire

(b)½ Upon the death of my said brother, Walter Dukenfield and my said sister, Adel C. Smith and the said Carlotta Monti (Montejo), I direct that my executors procure the organization of a membership or other approved corporation under the name of W. C. FIELDS COLLEGE for orphan white boys and girls, where no religion of any sort is to be preached. Harmony is the purpose of this thought. It is my desire the college will be built in California in Los Angeles County.

(c) I wish to disinherit anyone who in any way tries to confuse or break this will or who contributes in any way to break this will.

(d) I hereby nominate, constitute and appoint Magda Michael to be the executor of this, my last will and testament.

I also wish to bequeath to my friend, Goerge Moran, formerly of Moran and Mack, the sum of One Thousand Dollars.

IN WITNESS WHEREOF, I have hereunto set my hand this 28th day of April 1943.

      William C. Fields X
      WILLIAM C. FIELDS
       TESTATOR

The foregoing Will consisting of five (5) pages, including this one, was signed and subscribed by the said William C. Fields, the person named therein, at Los Angeles California, on the 28th day of April, 1943, in the presence of us, and each of us at the same time, and was at the time of his so subscribing the same acknowledged and declared by him to us to be his last Will and Testament, and thereupon we, at his request, and in his presence, and in the presence of each other, subscribed our names as witnesses thereto

TENTH: I hereby nominate and appoint my brother, DAVID NELSON of Los Angeles, California as the executor of this will. I direct that no bond be required for his services hereunder. I authorize him to compromise any claim for or against my estate and to sell any asset of my estate at any time without the authority of the court. Should my brother be unable to act as executor for whatever reason, I hereby nominate and appoint my friend GREG McDONALD as the executor of this will, also to act without bond.

ELEVENTH: I have intentionally and with full knowledge thereof, omitted to provide for any heirs or other individuals I may leave surviving. In the event that any such person should contest this will, then in such event, I give, devise and bequeath to said person the sum of $1.00 (one dollar) and no more.

IN WITNESS WHEREOF, I have hereunto set my hand this 22nd day of August, 1985.

Eric H. Nelson
ERIC H. NELSON

EIGHTH: If any legatee or beneficiary under this will or the trust agreement between myself as Grantor and YOKO ONO LENNON and ELI GARBER as Trustees, dated November 12, 1979 shall interpose objections to the probate of this Will, or institute or prosecute or be in any way interested or instrumental in the institution or prosecution of any action or proceeding for the purpose of setting aside or invalidating this Will, then and in each such case, I direct that such legatee or beneficiary shall receive nothing whatsoever under this Will or the aforementioned Trust.

IN WITNESS WHEREOF, I have subscribed and sealed and do publish and declare these presents as and for my Last Will and Testament, this 12th day of November, 1979.

_____(L.S.)

THE FOREGOING INSTRUMENT consisting of four (4) typewritten pages, including this page, was on the 12th day of November, 1979, signed, sealed, published and declared by JOHN WINSTON ONO LENNON, the Testator therein named, as and for his Last Will and Testament, in the present of us, who at his request, and in his presence, and in the presence of each other, have hereunto set our names as witnesses.

instrument to be my Last Will and Testament, this __3__ day
of __MARCH__, ~~1976~~. _1977_

Elvis A. Presley
ELVIS A. PRESLEY

      The foregoing instrument, consisting of this and eleven
(11) preceding typewritten pages, was signed, sealed, published
and declared by ELVIS A. PRESLEY, the Testator, to be his Last
Will and Testament, in our presence, and we, at his request and
in his presence and in the presence of each other, have hereunto
subscribed our names as witnesses, this __3__ day of __MARCH__
~~1976~~, at Memphis, Tennessee. _1977_

Ginger Alden   residing at _4152 Royal Crest Place_

Charles F. Hodge   residing at _3764 Elvis Presley Blvd_
Ann Dewey Smith   _2237 Court Avenue_

ATE OF TENNESSEE)

𝕷𝖆𝖘𝖙 𝖂𝖎𝖑𝖑 𝖆𝖓𝖉 𝕿𝖊𝖘𝖙𝖆𝖒𝖊𝖓𝖙

of

JAMES D. MORRISON

I, JAMES D. MORRISON, being of sound and disposing mind, memory and understanding, and after consideration for all persons, the objects of my bounty, and with full knowledge of the nature and extent of my assets, do hereby make, publish and declare this my Last Will and Testament, as follows:

FIRST: I declare that I am a resident of Los Angeles County, California; that I am unmarried and have no children.

SECOND: I direct the payment of all debts and expenses of last illness.

THIRD: I do hereby devise and bequeath each and every thing of value of which I may die possessed, including real property, personal property and mixed properties to PAMELA S. COURSON of Los Angeles County.

In the event the said PAMELA S. COURSON should predecease me, or fail to survive for a period of three months following the date of my death, then and in such event, the devise and bequest to her shall fail and the same is devised and bequeathed instead to my brother, ANDREW MORRISON of Monterey, California, and to my sister, ANNE R. MORRISON of Coronado Beach, California, to share and share alike; provided, however, further that in the event either of them should predecease me, then and in such event, the devise and bequest shall go to the other.

FOURTH: I do hereby appoint PAMELA S. COURSON and MAX FINK, jointly, Executors, or Executor and Executrix, as the case may be, of my estate, giving to said persons, and each of them, full power of appointment of substitution in their place and stead by their Last Will and Testament, or otherwise.

In the event said PAMELA S. COURSON shall survive me and be living at the time of her appointment, then in such event, bond is hereby waived.

I subscribe my name to this Will this _12_ day of February, 1969, at Beverly Hills, California.

JAMES D. MORRISON

ARTICLE XIII

It is my intention that no interest be paid on any of the
acies provided for in this Last Will or in any Codicil.

ARTICLE XIV

I desire that my remains be cremated, and that there be
formal services to note my passing.

I subscribe my name to this Will this   26th   day of
ember   , 1984, at Beverly Hills,   California.

ADMITTED TO PROBATE

Date **JAN 1 6 1987**

FRANK ZOLIN-COUNTY, Clerk Clerk

By _____ Deputy

CARY GRANT

FIRST CODICIL

TO LAST WILL AND TESTAMENT DATED AUGUST 18, 1981

OF

ROY H. FITZGERALD (a/k/a ROCK HUDSON)

I, ROY H. FITZGERALD, also known as ROCK HUDSON, a resident of the County of Los Angeles, State of California, do hereby make, publish and declare this to be the First Codicil to my Last Will and Testament which bears the date of August 18, 1981.

FIRST: I hereby delete in its entirety Article FOURTH of my said Last Will and Testament. I purposely make no provision for the benefit of TOM H. CLARK.

SECOND: As amended by this Codicil, I hereby ratify, confirm and republish my Last Will and Testament dated August 18, 1981.

IN WITNESS WHEREOF, I sign, seal, publish and declare this as a First Codicil to my Last Will and Testament dated August 18, 1981, in the presence of the persons witnessing it, at my request on this 23 day of August, 1984.

Roy H. Fitzgerald AKA Roy H. Fitzgerald

TENTH: It is my intention to make no provision
herein for my son Christopher or my daughter Christina for
reasons which are well known to them.

ELEVENTH: I direct that my remains be cremated.

IN WITNESS WHEREOF, I have hereunto set my hand and
seal this 28th day of October, 1976.

Joan Crawford Steele

SIGNED, SEALED, PUBLISHED AND DECLARED
by JOAN CRAWFORD STEELE, the Testatrix,
as and for her Last Will and Testament,

NINETEENTH: If any person who, under the p[...]ons of this my Will, would otherwise be entitled to any g[...] quest or devise or to any interest in the principal or inco[...] ny portion of my estate or of any trust established here[...] all file any objection to the probate of this my Will or [...] n any way contest such probate or initiate any litigati[...] t[...] ur- pose of which is to prevent the probate of this my Wil[...] set aside the probate of this my Will, then such person sh[...] such event, forfeit any and all such gift, devise, bequest [...] erest and the same shall be disposed of as if such person ha[...] ceased me.

IN WITNESS WHEREOF, I have subscribed and se[...] d do publish and declare these presents as and for my Last W[...] d Testament, in the presence of the witnesses attesting t[...] e at my request, this *22nd* day of *September* , Ninete[...] dred and Fifty-eight.

Jean Paul Getty

I, JEAN PAUL GETTY, of Santa Monica, California, do hereby make, publish and declare this to be a Codicil to my Last Will and Testament, dated September 22, 1958.

FIRST: I hereby amend my Last Will and Testament, dated September 22, 1958, by adding, following subdivision "(c)" of Article "SIXTH" of my said last Will and Testament, a new sub-division "(d)" to Article "SIXTH" of my said Last Will and Testament, which subdivision "(d)" shall read as follows:

(d) I give and bequeath to PENELOPE ANN KITSON, if she shall survive me, Two Thousand Five Hundred (2,500) shares of the common stock, as constituted at the time of my death, of Getty Oil Company or of such corporation as may result from any merger or consolidation, during my lifetime, of said Getty Oil Company and any other corporation or corporations or to which said Getty Oil Company may transfer substantially all its assets during my lifetime.

IN WITNESS WHEREOF, I have hereunto subscribed my name and affixed my seal to this, a Codicil to my Last Will and Testament dated September 22, 1958, this 18th day of June One Thousand Nine Hundred and Sixty.

 J. Paul Getty (L.S.)

"(2) To <u>PENELOPE ANN KITSON</u> the sum of
One Thousand One Hundred and Sixty-seven
($1,167) Dollars monthly as long as she shall
live."

    <u>SECOND</u>: Except as hereinabove modified, I here[by r]atify
and confirm my said Last Will and Testament dated Septem[ber] 22,
1958, as amended by a Codicil dated June 18, 1960 and a [Codi]cil
dated November 4, 1962, a Third Codicil dated December 2[0, 1]962,
a Fourth Codicil dated January 15, 1963, a Fifth Codicil[date]d
March 6, 1963, a Sixth Codicil dated September 16, 1965, [a]
Seventh Codicil dated March 11, 1966, an Eighth Codicil [dated]
January 5, 1967, a Ninth Codicil dated November 3, 1967 [and a]
Tenth Codicil dated February 24, 1969, and as so altered [and]
amended I hereby again publish and declare my said Will [and]
Codicils to be my Last Will and Testament.

    <u>IN WITNESS WHEREOF</u>, I have hereunto subscribed [my name]
and affixed my seal to this, an Eleventh Codicil to my s[aid]
Will and Testament, this **18**th day of **March** One Th[ousand]
Nine Hundred and Sixty-nine.

<u>Jean Paul Getty</u>

John Cassavetes
and
Phil Silvers

The entirely handwritten Wills of director John Cassavetes and comedian Phil Silvers are stark, to the point, and quite revealing about the most intimate thoughts of these two men.

June 3, 1988

I, John Cassavetes, being of sound mind, and living at 7917 Woodrow Wilson Drive Los Angeles 90046. Cal. do hereby declare My Last Will and Testament as follows:

I leave all and every thing I own or will own to my beloved wife. Gena Rowlands Cassavetes.

I leave nothing to anyone else, whomsoever, they may be.

I owe noone any debt or obligation, other than usual and ordinary bills.

No one has done me a special service that I feel obligated to.

I hereby appoint my wife, Gena Executor of this will. She may at her discretion appoint another executor -

John Cassavetes
June 3, 1988

This document, my only valid will replaces any previous will that might have been drawn. and has been witnessed by my attorney, James Cohen. and my secretary, Doe Avedon Siegel both of Los Angeles, Cal. Enclosed their witness document. - JC John Cassavetes June 3, 1988 —

1

Phil Silvers (July 4th 1984)

This handwritten document will serve as my last will and testament

I request for David Glynn of the firm of Treubner & Glynn to share the duties of Executor with my eldest daughter Tracey

For carrying out my requests they are to receive and share the sum of Five Thousand dollars $2500 each

— Executing the following requests I leave my entire fortune to be shared equally by my five daughters namely

Tracey, Nancy, Cathy, Candace and Laury, This legacy includes my ownerships of all Stocks and Bonds. Bank accounts, securities and monies in Banks and possible partial ownership such as the Television series "Gilligan Island". My many awards and documents, photos, and memorabilia should be shared equally by my five above mentioned daughters, this is to be supervised by my eldest child Tracey

my further request

To my sister Mrs Pearl Saben of 200 W 59th St New York City × 10019

the sum of Fifteen Thousand dollars $15,000

To my brother Bob Silver 1130 Brighton Beach Ave Brooklyn, N.Y. 1235

Fifteen thousand Dollars 1500

In the event both the above my Brother and sister are not alive to accept this legacy both sums $30,000 Thirty thousand in Total should be awarded my Nephew Saul Silver

390 First Ave
New York City
N.Y. 10010

Phil Silvers

To. My friend Leo de Lyon 13147 Hartland Cir. N.
Hollywood. Ca 91605 To him I bequest the sum of Five
Thousand dollars $5000 and with this sum my deep respect and
love — To my nurse and constant companion

Mr. Jean Edward
109 348 Eucalyptus.
apt E
Hawthorne
Ca 90250

phone no: 978-5939

I bequeath to mrs Edwards the sum of Five
Thousand Dollars $5000 small payment for her
many considerations during my long illness

I have made no reference to my ex wife Evelyn Patrick
early in our marriage there were some years and there are
five children will attest however for reasons best to the both
of us I leave her nothing material in my also no bitterness
at this writing she is doing very well is her well prepared
profession and I wish her well

Any reference to the validity of my mental alertness
can be attested by my Doctor of many years

Clarence M Agress 353-2021 he kept me going when
my physical condition was shaky following a stroke in 1973

I request my daughter Tracey to inform the
medies of my passing and to arrange my funeral
in Forest Lawn I want a simple coffin and a small
stone Phil Silvers Comedian

I expect David Glynn and TRACY to inform the media and if possible I would appreciate a small eulogue delivered by my friend of many years Milton Berle. I request my funeral arrangement coffin and head stone not to exceed the sum of Ten thousand dollars $10,000

Good by I go to my rest willingly The last years were painful but were made bearable by friends I made through the years especially Ed Trautner who smoothed out many a curve

I go to my god knowing at least as a comedian I was one of a kind

Shalom

Phil

August 15 · 1985

I leave to my daughters, Tracy + Nancy my apartment, 1905. in the west building of the Century Tower 2220 ave. of the stars.

All the contents of my apartment shall be divided furniture, photos, awards, equally between them

If they so desire they shall share some of the above with their sisters Cathy, Candy and Laury

I love them all

Phil Silvers

Glossary of Legal Terms

*E*ntire books or volumes of books have been written about the meanings and intricacies of each of the following legal words or phrases. For the purposes of this compendium of Wills, the following simplified definitions should help the reader to understand their usage in this text, but should not be relied upon for any sophisticated legal analysis.

Bequeath—To give a gift of personal property (as opposed to real property) to a person or institution by Will.

Bequest—A gift of personal property (as opposed to real property) made pursuant to a Will.

Codicil—A written and witnessed document that supplements, revokes, or alters certain provisions of a Will and that is executed after the date of the Will, but with all the same formalities.

Conservator—A person appointed by the court to manage and handle the affairs of an incompetent person. A conservator is often appointed as a result of a *conservatorship proceeding* brought before a court.

Construction Proceeding—Case that is brought in court to interpret and apply Will provisions that are unclear or ambiguous.

Copyright—A person's ownership rights in original works authored or created by that person as long as they are fixed in any tangible medium of expression; applies to musical, literary, or visual works.

Devise—A gift of real property (as opposed to personal property) made pursuant to a Will. *Devise* may also be used as a noun to describe the real property that has been gifted. A person or institution that receives the devise is a *devisee*.

Estate—The quantity and nature of the real property (i.e., land and buildings) and personal property, whether intangible (e.g., stocks, bonds, or partnership interests) or tangible (e.g., chairs, paintings, or automobiles), that a person owns or has an interest in. The aggregate of all that is called a person's estate when he or she dies. The word is often applied to the living, who might be doing some estate-planning and preparing for the inevitable.

Executor—Person designated in a Will to administer the estate and to execute the terms of the Will.

Heir—Technically, the person who would inherit the estate if there were no Will; next of kin. *Heir* is often used informally to describe the person who actually inherited part or all of an estate pursuant to a Will.

In Terrorem Clause—*In terrorem* is Latin for "in fright or terror." Used in a Will an *in terrorem* clause threatens the forfeiture of a beneficiary's bequest or interest under a Will should that beneficiary contest the validity of the Will—and lose his suit. Such clauses come in a variety of forms and often do not deter a person from contesting the Will.

Inter Vivos Trust—Trust established by a person during that person's life.

Intestate—Dying without a valid Will. The condition of dying without a valid Will is referred to as *intestacy*.

Last Will and Testament—A written and witnessed document in which a person designates executors, guardians, and/or trustees to administer and dispose of his or her real and/or personal property after his or her death and to take care of family members and others in the manner specified.

Letters of Administration—Certificate issued by the court confirming its appointment of a person, persons, or an institution to administer an estate when the decedent left no valid Will.

Letters of Trusteeship—Certificate issued by a court confirming its appointment of a person, persons, and/or an institution to act as the trustee or trustees of a trust.

Letters Testamentary—Certificate issued by a court confirming its acceptance of a person, persons, or an institution named in a Will to execute the terms of the Will in accordance with the applicable law.

Per Capita—Latin for "by the heads of polls"; method of distribution of estate property when it is made to persons, each of whom is to take in his own right an equal portion of such property.

Per Stirpes—Latin for "by roots or stocks"; method of distribution of estate property when it is made to persons who take as issue, in equal portions, the share that their deceased ancestor would have taken if living.

Primogeniture—Anglo-Saxon concept of law whereby the eldest son has the primary right to succeed to his ancestor's estate.

Probate—Procedure whereby a court accepts the proof of an instrument as the decedent's Last Will and Testament. When the court accepts the validity of such instrument, "the Will had been admitted to probate." The word *probate* also popularly applies to the entire process of an estate administration.

Remainder—The portion of a trust or estate that is left after any life beneficiaries of such trust or estate have died, or their life interest has otherwise terminated. The remainder is a future interest, contingent or vested, of a third party other than the grantor of the property.

Residuary estate—Term used to describe what amount of a person's estate remains for division after the payment of the decedent's and the estate's debts and expenses and any *pre-residuary bequests* or *devises* made in the Will. What is left is divided by the *residuary beneficiaries*.

Testamentary Trust—A trust established under a Will or "testament" of old.

Testate—Dying with a valid Will.

Testator—A male who signs a valid Will.

Testatrix—A female who signs a valid Will.

Trust—An arrangement whereby property is transferred to trustees to be held for the benefit of another person, or other persons or institutions. If the property is transferred pursuant to instructions in a Will, that is a testamentary trust. If the property has been transferred during the life of the grantor or settlor, that is an *inter vivos* trust.

Trustee—Person named in an *inter vivos* trust or under a Will to administer the trust according to its terms.

Will—If you do not know what a Will is by now, you should return to the beginning of this book.

Index